Meditation *for* Wimps

MEDITATION

for WIMPS

FINDING YOUR

BALANCE IN

AN IMPERFECT

WORLD

Miriam Austin

Photography by Barry Kaplan

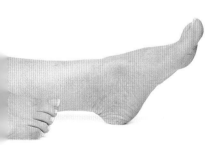

STERLING PUBLISHING CO., INC.
NEW YORK

May we all be free from suffering.
May we all be at peace.
May we all enjoy great happiness.
May we all love, accept, and care for one another.
May we all live in eternal bliss.

Art direction and design by Lubosh Cech *okodesignstudio.com*
Photography by Barry Kaplan

Library of Congress Cataloging-in-Publication Data Available

10 9 8 7 6 5 4 3 2 1

Published by Sterling Publishing Co., Inc.
387 Park Avenue South, New York, N.Y. 10016
©2003 by Miriam Austin
Distributed in Canada by Sterling Publishing
$^{c}/o$ Canadian Manda Group, One Atlantic Avenue, Suite 105
Toronto, Ontario, Canada M6K 3E7
Distributed in Great Britain by Chrysalis Books
64 Brewery Road, London N7 9NT, England
Distributed in Australia by Capricorn Link (Australia) Pty. Ltd.
P.O. Box 704, Windsor, NSW 2756, Australia

Printed in China

Sterling ISBN 0-8069-6917-2

You can visit Miriam Austin at her website:
www.yogaforwimps.com

Acknowledgments

This book has been created over the course of my entire life, and so there are many, many people to thank for their influence. First, I thank my parents, Richard and Betty Hammer, who through their own devotion to God and by their example of charity and generosity started me on this path. Then I have to thank life itself, for all of the troubles it has presented me — because without those troubles, I'm not sure I would have found this path or followed it so fervently. When my life has been upside down, some of my dear friends taught me many of the meditations you find in this book — Nancy Stechert, Gayle Pierce, David Bierman, and Patrick Tribble.

I have had many teachers who through their books have touched me deeply — His Holiness the Dalai Lama, Chogyam Trungpa Rinpoche, Pema Chodron, Thich Nhat Hahn, Lao Tzu, Geri Larkin, Stephen and Ondrea Levine, Rabbi Joseph Gelberman, Rabbi Aryeh Kaplan, St. Theresa of Avila, St. John of the Cross, Thomas Merton, and many other Christian mystics.

I have had the good fortune to spend time with some truly wise and compassionate spiritual teachers. Sri Sri Ravi Shankar, known to his students as Punditji, is the founder of the Art of Living Foundation. Punditji insists that his students seek the Divine within themselves and gives them unique breathing and meditation techniques to accelerate that process. Amrita Anandamayi, affectionately known as Ammachi, is the epitome of joy, love, and compassion. She travels around the world, loving and soothing those who seek her blessing. Additionally, through their charitable organizations, Punditji and Ammachi feed, clothe, house, educate, and provide medical care for many thousands of people around the world. I was lucky enough to very casually meet and spend some time with Kunzig Shamar Rinpoche, the present Sharmapa of the Karma Kaygu Buddhist tradition. It wasn't until a few years later, when I became steeped in Buddhism in his tradition, that I realized how auspicious our meeting was.

I am blessed to work with the most wonderful Catholic priests — The Marians of the Immaculate Conception. All aspects of my life are greatly enriched through my work with them and through the community's devotion to Christ as Divine Mercy Incarnate and to the Blessed Mother.

My daily example of patience, kindness, compassion, joy, and love is my husband, Van. Van is the embodiment of these virtues and is a continual inspiration.

Naturally, I want to express my gratitude to everyone at Sterling Publishing. I particularly want to thank my insightful editor, Steve Magnuson, for his guidance, enthusiasm, and friendship. Thanks to Charlie Nurnberg and Lincoln Boehm for giving me a forum for expressing my ideas. Great thanks to Barry Kaplan for his beautiful photography and to Lubosh Cech for his magnificent design. Thanks to Danielle Truscott and Isabel Stein for their diligent efforts. My gratitude extends to the dozens of people at Sterling, most of whom I have never met, who spent many long hours working on this book.

In writing this book, I have been lucky enough to have had the opportunity to deepen my meditation practice. But I have always been lucky and I have always felt incredibly blessed. I am eternally grateful to the Divine Power that has bestowed upon me such good fortune.

Contents

1

2

Author's Preface

This book is, in a sense, an autobiography of my experiences with meditation. Meditation was a natural offspring of my yoga practice, which I started in the mid-1980s. At first, yoga and meditation were simply ways to de-stress from my high-pressure career. As my life unfolded, with all of its accompanying challenges, I was fortunate enough to find many friends who were much farther down the meditation path than I. I'm thankful that they taught me many different ways to meditate that helped with the various challenges life dealt me. My friends taught me how to calm my fears and my anger, how to deal with uncomfortable situations, and how to foster understanding, acceptance, and compassion for myself and for others.

As my practice grew, I became more and more interested in the spiritual aspect of meditation. I read many books and participated in dozens of meditation retreats. Writing this book was a challenge: what to include was easy, but what to leave out was a struggle.

This book is designed as an introduction to meditation. My intention is to give you a sample or taste of many different meditation practices. This book gives you specific restorative yoga postures so you can immediately and effortlessly relax. It also gives methods for quieting your mind and ways to resolve negative feelings. My intention is to help you reduce stress and to nurture your finest qualities: love, kindness, forgiveness, compassion, gentleness, serenity, peace, and joy. In that context, I think this book is complete.

There are hundreds of books that are more comprehensive discussions of meditation, particularly of meditation's spiritual traditions. Here I give you a taste of meditations from several different faiths. In doing so, I am not advocating one spiritual path over another. I believe that we are all looking for something "supreme" in our lives; meditation, more than anything else, satisfies the hunger for that something supreme. Meditation and spirituality are deep, vast, and in many ways indescribable, so we each must find our own path and ultimately trust our own experience.

As for me, I satisfied my spiritual longings by studying the writings of various traditions and by practicing their meditation techniques. My study has greatly enriched my experience. Although I come from a Christian background, I found that experiencing different spiritual paths has given me insights I did not find in my own tradition. In studying the teachings and practicing the meditations from other paths, I gained a fuller understanding of Christ's message. I have found that the essence of all religions is the same, but because each tradition emphasizes specific elements, studying more than one path clarifies the broader message.

My experience of meditation has been like making a quilt. Just as different patterns of cloth that are carefully chosen and sewn together result in a beautiful quilt, I have interwoven different secular and spiritual practices to make my own experience whole, full, and extraordinarily beautiful. Once you have found some peace from your hectic life and resolved certain challenges through meditation, I invite you to try some of the meditations from your own spiritual tradition and some from traditions that are different from your own. As we experience spiritual teachings from all corners of the world, we learn that all spiritual wisdom emanates from the same source, and we soon learn why all of the spiritual traditions advise us to look for that source within our own heart.

What Is a Wimp?

Those of you who read my last book, *Yoga for Wimps,* will remember that the title came from an ongoing sibling rivalry. When I started taking yoga classes in the mid-1980s, Mike, my very athletic brother, often teased, "Yoga? Yoga's for wimps!" Of course, he wouldn't try any poses, so I called him a wimp back and said that one day I would write a book just for him. Fourteen years later, *Yoga for Wimps* was published and met with great international success. Why such great success? Certainly because yoga has become extremely popular, but also because everyone I talk to can relate to being a wimp.

We're all wimps in some way. We wimps are often tempted to wimp out on life's many commitments. How often do we want to pull the covers up over our heads instead of going to work on a rainy day (or even on a sunny day)? How often do we feel as though we just can't take on another project at work, or feel like we need a vacation although we just got back from one? Can't we just wimp out on washing the car, mowing the lawn,

working out at the gym, going to the company Christmas party? Often we wimp out not because we don't truly want to do these things, but because we're too overwhelmed with everything else we have to do. We need some time alone to rest and recover.

Meditation for Wimps is designed to do just that: provide the rest and relaxation we all need to fulfill our commitments with equanimity and enthusiasm. Keeping in mind the limited amount of time you have, *Meditation for Wimps* helps you get started by providing the most effective and effortless ways to meditate. It gives practical advice for dealing with life's inevitable ups and downs and helps you recover from stress, anxiety, and depression. *Meditation for Wimps* restores you by connecting you with your wisest, most loving, kindest, and most compassionate self. It simplifies and demystifies meditation.

Where do we go from here? Get your pillows and blankets ready. You'll be amazed at how quickly and easily you will be meditating.

What Is Meditation and Why Do It?

Webster's definition of meditation is "to focus one's thoughts; to reflect or ponder over something; to plan or project in the mind." The word *meditate* comes from the Latin word *mederi,* which means "to remedy." *Dhyana* is the term for meditation in Sanskrit, the ancient Indian language that is used in the Hindu tradition and in some Buddhist traditions. Dhyana translates to "prolonged one-pointed attention."

In traditional meditation, we focus our prolonged one-pointed attention on a prayer, a mantra, or on our breath. By doing this, we redirect our mind from the usual thoughts of reviewing the past or planning the future to the present moment. Practicing meditation restores us, ultimately giving us a calm, quiet mind both during our practice time and throughout our day.

Meditation can also be defined as any practice or discipline we undertake to restore ourselves physically, emotionally, mentally, and spiritually. Meditation can be anything that enriches our lives, prepares us for our activities, helps us become more calm and centered, focuses our attention, heightens our self-awareness, increases our spiritual awareness, or connects us to whatever it is we consider supreme in our lives.

In my experience, most people start a formal or traditional meditation practice as a means to relax and regain their balance, which is often lost in the course of their daily activities. Stress fatigues the body and the mind. It cuts us off from our innate goodness, joy, and inner love. If we are tired and stressed, it is easier to get angry, to be fearful, to envy, or to be generally discontented. Our patience runs thinnest and our relationships suffer the most when we are exhausted, worried, and anxious.

It is no surprise that harmonizing ourselves and returning to our natural state of goodness is an essential aspect of meditation. We often need to heal and renew ourselves. We need an antidote for our physical, mental, and emotional stress. Our lives are often more upside down than right side up. We can use meditation to turn things around physically, mentally, and emotionally. Calming our stress and soothing our nerves are meditation's most tangible and immediate benefits.

On a physiological level, meditation normalizes many of the body's functions by:

- calming and stabilizing the nervous system

- decreasing cortisol, the body's primary stress hormone

- reducing muscle tension

- normalizing blood pressure

- reducing serum cholesterol

- increasing serotonin, a neuro-transmitter often associated with happiness.

Because meditation helps us become calmer on the physiological level, we are then mentally, emotionally, and spiritually more tranquil. As we experience more inner peace, we feel more alive. When difficulties arise, we are able to meet them with equanimity and grace instead of with worry and fear. And as our sense of joy and inner peace amplifies, it is easier for us to express our innate love, kindness, patience, wisdom, and compassion. At our innermost core, which we connect to through meditation, we find that these finer qualities are our true nature.

As we uncover, nurture, and stay connected to our highest qualities through meditation, we find that we are aligned with what all spiritual paths encourage — becoming our best self. The meditative techniques in each tradition differ. They include prayer, mantra repetition, following or controlling the breath, singing, dancing, and yoga exercises. Yet the techniques are a means to a common end: quieting the mind. By quieting our minds through meditation, we become more aware of the nature of our own minds and our connection to the cosmos. Through meditation, we connect with our core consciousness, which is infinitely

loving, kind, joyful, serene, wise, forgiving, and compassionate. Through meditation, we allow God to more fully manifest within us. We discover and uncover our own Divine potential. Most Christians call this core consciousness the Holy Spirit, Christ consciousness, or the soul. Buddhists call it Buddha Nature or emptiness. Taoists call it the *Tao* or the mystery. Jews call it *ayin*. Muslims call it Perfection. Hindus call it Brahman. What we call the experience does not matter; what we experience does.

Although you may begin a meditation practice as a way to reduce stress, you are most likely to experience something wonderful that is beyond your ordinary existence. As you continue to meditate, you will find that this experience will filter into all aspects of your life. Negative habits start to drop by the wayside, relationships improve, joy multiplies. This feeling of well-being is addictive — you will soon find that you are setting aside time to meditate each day.

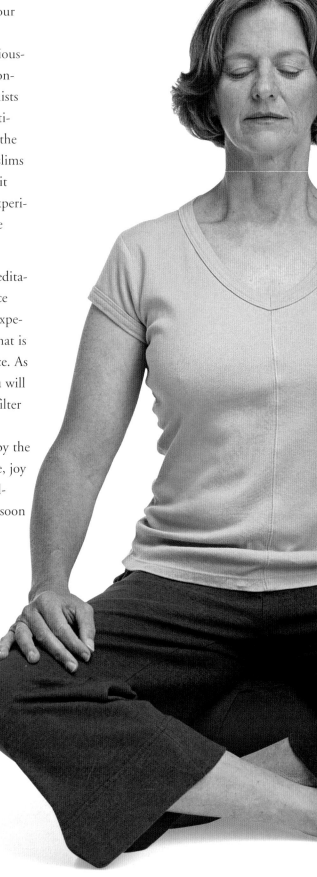

How to Use This Book

As a self-professed wimp, I know that most of us don't read "how-to" books from cover to cover. In fact, most of us don't even read the *Getting Started* section until we have questions about something specific. If you fall into this category, but find yourself actually reading this How-to section, I would like to suggest an easy, effective way to use this book.

First, scan the *Instant Meditation* section. In this section, look for meditation postures you want to try. Be sure to use several of the restorative yoga poses found there. You will adore them! Then more carefully go through *Quieting the Mind, Fix-Its,* and *Going Deeper.* Pick out a technique or a meditation and combine your favorite posture with the meditation.

Continue this process of choosing a posture and a meditation until you have tried all of your top choices. Then choose a few meditations that you would not normally try, just to see if there are any benefits you can glean from them. You just might be surprised.

When you start to have questions or want to understand a specific term, go to the *Getting Started* section.

Above all, allow your experience of this book to be playful and exploratory. Do not get stressed about doing everything perfectly. Don't worry if you can't keep your mind on your meditation. Just bring your awareness back when you realize that your mind has drifted. Don't feel inadequate if you get sleepy. Meditation calms you on a very deep level, so you may want to take a nap instead of finishing the meditation. And that's okay.

Remember, this is *Meditation for Wimps.* There are no hard and fast rules. If later you decide you want more rules, there is plenty of time for that. For now, let your inner wisdom be your guide to this new adventure in meditation.

The impulse to meditate is so powerful in all of us that you have probably meditated many times without realizing it. For example, we all have tried to prepare for difficult situations by "collecting our thoughts" or making a plan. We've all taken time out to soothe ourselves by watching a stream or a beautiful sunset and have found ourselves calm, peaceful, and restored. We have all gotten "lost" in projects and when we are "found," we are amazed at how much time has passed. However, if you are going to have a more formal practice of meditation, there are a few things you need to know, have, and do.

1

Getting Started

What You Need to Know

FAQs (FREQUENTLY ASKED QUESTIONS)

Many beginners have questions about the do's and don'ts of meditation. Listed below are a few of them, with answers that I have gleaned through my own experience meditating and teaching meditation. The answers to these questions are appropriate for *beginning* meditators. Other teachers and different meditation traditions may have different answers. As you progress in your own meditation practice, the right answers for you will become apparent.

How long should I meditate?

If you are using one of the lying down poses, you can stay in the pose and focus on the meditation for as long as you like. If you are sitting in a meditation posture, initially meditate for 3 or 4 minutes. As you progress, you can expand the time to 6 to 7 minutes, then 10 to 12 minutes, and when you feel ready, up to 20 to 30 minutes. Do not feel the need to force yourself to extend the time period; gradually increase the time.

Can I move during meditation, or do I have to be perfectly still?

In meditation, you naturally want to be as still as possible. However, for a beginner this might be difficult, so if your nose itches, scratch it. If you need to move to get more comfortable, do so. The one caution I would give is this: when you move during meditation, move with as much awareness of your action as possible. Make the movement part of your meditation.

What if I am interrupted for some reason and have to stop my meditation?

If the doorbell rings or your child interrupts you, attend to the situation and then go back to your meditation. If you don't have the opportunity to continue the meditation, at least lie down for a few minutes when you return from the disruption.

Can I meditate anywhere?

Ideally, a quiet place in your home is recommended. But you can meditate anywhere — in a church or temple, in a park, in your office to help you de-stress and refocus, or while on an airplane, bus, or train. You might try a pair of earplugs for the noisier venues.

What can I expect during meditation?

Everyone's experience is different. The best thing to do is to simply follow the instructions for the particular meditation and be open to the possibilities.

What if I can't stop thinking while I meditate?

Thoughts are a natural part of meditation. There are different ways of dealing with your thoughts, depending on the tradition you practice. Don't be overly concerned about the mind wandering. Thoughts are part of the process. Most meditation traditions teach that when you realize that you are thinking, gently bring your mind back to your mantra, your prayer, or your breath. Some meditation masters say that we must go through all of the thoughts in order to get to the quiet mind. Others say that we must simply observe our thoughts, without attaching to them or judging them. Whichever method you choose, eventually the mind will quiet down. You will continue to have thoughts, but your mind will generally be much calmer.

COMMON TERMS

There are many terms related to meditation that you may have heard without being quite sure what they mean. Listed below are definitions of some of those terms.

- Awareness: Through meditation, we become more and more conscious of our thoughts, movements, and behavior. Increased awareness leads to insights about ourselves and the nature of our minds. As we become more conscious of our own natures, we gain insight into others and into life itself.

- Enlightenment: The literal definition is "to bring into the light." The term *enlightenment* normally refers to the state in which individual consciousness merges with cosmic consciousness.

- Flow: A term popularized by Professor Mihaly Csikzentmihaly. *Flow* refers to the mental state in which one is completely focused and absorbed in the activity at hand and is unaware of either time or surroundings.

- Guru: A guru is a teacher. *Guru* means "one who brings you from darkness into light." Gurus are normally associated with the Hindu path of spirituality. In some cases, the guru awakens the spiritual desire in the student. Most gurus are willing to initiate and guide a student, but ultimately the guru encourages his student to discipline himself to meditate regularly and to find the Divine within. It is not necessary to have a guru in order to meditate.

- Kundalini: The Sanskrit term for the life force, which is located at the base of the spine. Through yoga exercises, meditation, and other spiritual practices, the Kundalini energy moves up the spine and initiates enlightenment.

- Lotus Position (*padmasana* in Sanskrit): A yogic seated-meditation posture in which each foot is placed on top of the opposite thigh. This is an advanced yoga pose, requiring extraordinary flexibility in the hips, knees, and ankles. Forcing yourself into this pose can cause injury, so it should only be practiced by those who find it completely comfortable.

- Mantra: A sacred sound, word, phrase, or prayer that one concentrates on during meditation.

- Mindfulness: A state in which one is completely attentive and aware of each and every movement, thought, and breath in each and every moment. Unlike what happens in the flow state, a person practicing mindfulness is conscious of time and surroundings.

- Mudra: *Mudra* is Sanskrit for "seal" or "sign." In Hinduism and Buddhism, a mudra is a hand gesture that is a visible sign of a spiritual reality. Many people use mudras while meditating. There are dozens of mudras, and different schools of meditation use different ones. Described below are two of the simplest mudras.

1. The Mudra of Receptivity: The palms are open and the back of the hands rest on the knees or thighs if you are in a seated posture. If you are in a reclining meditation posture, the backs of the hands touch the floor. The Mudra of Receptivity reminds us to accept all of life as it comes to us. Opening our hands in this mudra is a symbolic gesture of surrendering to the Divine. If our hands are open, we can graciously accept the gifts the Universe wants to give us. Many of us habitually hold our hands tight, perhaps because we are afraid we will be given more suffering. Yet we must remember that in suffering our internal strengths are revealed, so along with the suffering we receive great gifts.

2. The Mudra of Interconnection: Placing the tips of the thumbs and the tips of the forefingers together performs this mudra. It reminds us that life is circular, that everything in life is connected.

- Nirvana: A Buddhist term for the extinguishing of worldly desires and attachments, leading to a state of bliss. The state in which individual consciousness merges with Cosmic Consciousness.

- OM: A fundamental mantra used in Hindu meditation and often used as part of a mantra in Buddhist meditation. OM is considered the sound of God or the sound of Universal Consciousness. The usual pronunciation is OH-M, but some-

times it is drawn out into three syllables: AH-OO-MM.

- Pranayama: *Prana* means "breath" in Sanskrit. *Pranayama* is the yogic discipline of controlled breathing. The practice helps prepare the body and mind for meditation. Pranayama can be done while sitting or lying down. When lying down, a pranayama pillow, which is available through yoga supply catalogues, is often used. Only very simple pranayama techniques are taught in this book.

- Third Eye (*dyoya-drsti* in Sanskrit): In the Hindu tradition, the third eye is located between, and very slightly above, the eyebrows. Many spiritual traditions teach that the third

eye is the seat of wisdom, inner light, and Divine insight.

- TM or Transcendental Meditation: A mantra-based meditation technique originally taught by Maharishi Mahesh Yogi, an Indian spiritual teacher. Starting in the late 1950s, Maharishi, as he is affectionately called by his students, popularized meditation in the West.

What You Need to Have

Essential Props

Depending on which postures you choose for meditation, you will need one or all of the following accessories:

- Four to six sturdy blankets
- A wooden yoga block or a dictionary-sized book
- Earplugs
- Eye covers, which could include a face towel, an Ace® bandage (see details below), or an eye cover with an elastic band that goes around the back of the head (available at most drugstores)
- 2 face towels
- Hand towel
- Pillow
- Chair

Additional Props

You may want to have additional props such as incense, bells, or meditational music. These items are used in many church services as well as by meditators.

- Incense: The fragrance of incense purifies the environment. The burning of the incense symbolizes the burning of the force that distracts the mind, thus allowing us to more fully concentrate on our meditation.
- Bell: The ringing of a bell during meditation or prayer eliminates distracting sounds and helps us concentrate on the meditation. There are many types of bells: standard bells, gongs, and cymbals.
- Music: For many of us, music raises the energy or vibration of the atmosphere. That's why there is so much spiritual music available. Choose something that is soothing and will help you focus your attention inward rather than outward toward the music.
- Candles: The lighting of candles is symbolic for the turning on of our inner light, our own divinity.
- Pranayama Pillow: A long, thin, firm pillow used for yogic breathing exercises (pranayama). They are available through yoga-supply catalogues.
- Ace Bandage: Standard Ace bandage, 4 inches (10 cm) in width, available at most drugstores.
- Zazen Bench: A meditation bench that helps keep the back straight and the knees comfortable. Available through most meditation-supply catalogues.

Preparing for Meditation

Set aside a particular place in your home that is quiet and serene. It is important to meditate in peaceful surroundings. However, if you live in an urban area with lots of noise and cannot naturally block out the noise, earplugs help. Naturally, you can meditate in a religious environment or in your favorite place in nature. You may also find that you can do some form of meditation as you go about your daily activities or as you go to sleep at night.

General Relaxation

A good way to prepare for meditation is to use this progressive relaxation technique. You progressively relax the body, moving from the feet to the head. During the relaxation process, you direct your breath into certain areas of the body, which allows your muscles to relax more readily. This is done by first focusing your mind on your feet. Then, taking a deep inhalation, imagine that you are inhaling and exhaling through your feet, rather than through your nose. Keep doing this, gradually moving up the legs, torso, arms, neck, and head. This technique relaxes your body and quiets your mind.

Another simple relaxation technique uses imagery. Imagine yourself lying on a blanket on the beach on a warm, sunny day. Your body is made of ice, and you are slowly melting into the blanket. As you relax your body, your mind will become quiet, thus preparing you for the full benefit of your chosen meditation.

- Choose one of the lying-down postures described on pages 26 to 37. Allow yourself to comfortably settle into the posture. Gently close your eyes or cover them. You can listen to some soothing music or you can use earplugs to help block out the external noise.

- With your eyes closed, allow your inward gaze to focus on your heart. Breathe deeply into your tummy. As you go through this technique, breathe into the part of the body you are trying to relax. Don't worry if you don't think it is working, just keep doing it. Soon you will realize that is has worked. All of your tension will have dissolved into the floor, the bed, or into the props you are using.

- Focus your attention on your feet, inhaling and exhaling into your feet for a few moments, allowing your feet, your toes, and your ankles to soften. Then move your attention and your breath to your shins, your calves, and your knees, allowing them to completely relax. Breathe into your thighs, softening and releasing your inner thighs and your outer thighs. Soften the top of the thighs and the back of the thighs. Imagine that your legs and feet have completely melted into the floor.

- Next, move your breath into your hips, allowing the hip muscles to soften and release. Move the breath into your lower back, softening and releasing your lower back muscles toward the floor. Soften your tummy, taking big belly breaths, softening and releasing the abdominal muscles. Taking deep breaths into your chest, soften your ribcage and your chest. Soften the very upper chest — releasing the front of the shoulders, the top of the shoulders, and the sides of the shoulders. Breathe into your lower back again, softening and releasing the lower back muscles. Bring the breath and the relaxation into your middle back, softening and releasing the back of the ribcage. Breathe into the upper back, releasing the shoulder blades and the area between the shoulder blades. Soften the very top of your back, releasing the back of the shoulders. Imagine that your torso has completely melted into the floor.

- Direct your breath into your arms, softening your upper arms and elbows, softening the forearms and the wrists. Breathe into your hands, releasing your palms and your fingers. Imagine that your arms and hands have completely melted into the floor.

- Breathe into your throat and sides of your neck, allowing them to completely soften. Breathe into the back of your neck. Allow all of your neck muscles to soften and release downward, dissolving all the tension.

- Breathe into your lower face, softening your jaw, your teeth, and your gums. Release all tension in your tongue. Breathing into your face, soften the skin on your face and soften your temples. Breathe into your eyes, softening your eyes and your eyelids. Allow your inward gaze to be toward your heart. Know that your heart is your center of wisdom, kindness, compassion, serenity, joy, and love. Recognize that these qualities are who you truly are. Take a moment to acknowledge your true nature.

- Breathe into your forehead, softening your forehead. Direct your breath into the head, softening the top of your head and the back of your head. Let your entire face and head soften, as though your head is melting into the floor.

- Once again, focus your inward gaze toward your heart. Breathe

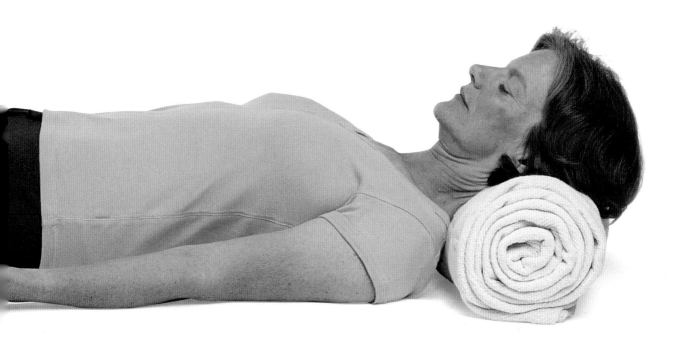

normally, without trying to control the breath. Focus on your breath, taking normal inhalations and normal exhalations. If your mind starts to wander, just bring your attention back to the breath. Allow your thoughts to come and go as easily as the breath comes and goes. Normal inhalations, followed by normal exhalations, inhaling everything that is necessary, exhaling everything that is unnecessary.

Standard Meditation Technique

In the *Instant Meditation* and *Quieting the Mind* chapters of the book, many postures and techniques are presented. You can use these for your meditation or you can use them to prepare for other meditations offered in *Fix-Its* and

in *Going Deeper*. If you are using meditations from the latter two sections of the book, here are some suggestions to enhance your experience. A variation of these instructions is given at the beginning of each meditation in *Fix-Its* and *Going Deeper*.

- Assume your favorite meditation posture, choosing one from the *Instant Meditation* section.

- In most of the meditation practices described in this book, you will gently close your eyes, releasing all tension from your eyes, and focus your inward gaze toward your heart. Focusing on your heart reminds you that your true nature is love, kindness, and compassion and that your true nature resides in your heart.

- Many of the meditations suggest that you "make an intention"

prior to practice. For example, if you are practicing one of the compassion meditations, it may say: "Make the intention that you are practicing this meditation to increase compassion for yourself and for others." Making an intention helps you focus your consciousness in the direction in which you would like to grow.

- Focus your attention on your breath for a minute or two to help relax your body and quiet your mind.

- Now you are ready to practice the specific meditation.

- If you are using a mantra or prayer meditation, try to coordinate your breath with the words. Specific examples are given with each meditation.

A WORD ABOUT THE BREATH

The breath is of paramount importance to our well-being. When we are under stress, we often stop breathing or our breathing becomes shallow, so our body doesn't get the oxygen it needs, thus causing more stress.

In meditation, we become aware of our breath. We can use it to relax our bodies and quiet our minds.

We learn that being aware of our breath helps keep us in the present moment. Some meditation practices solely focus on the breath; some of those are presented here. Most meditations suggest that you combine a mantra, phrase, or prayer with your breathing. As you practice various meditations, try to maintain awareness of your breath.

You will inevitably lose track of your breath; that is part of the process. But each time you find your mind wandering, bring your attention back to your breath and, if appropriate, back to your mantra, phrase, or prayer.

THE ACE BANDAGE TECHNIQUE

In any of the restorative yoga poses or sitting meditation postures, try using an Ace bandage wrapped around your head. The bandage helps block out noise and light. It helps you focus internally by closing the most powerful senses of perception, the eyes and ears. The pressure of the bandage can also help ease headaches and sinus problems.

- Start with the Ace bandage rolled up and your eyes closed.

- Take the end and place it between your eyebrows, covering part of the bridge of your nose and part of your forehead.

- Holding the end with one hand, partially unroll the bandage and cover one eye.

- Wrap the bandage around the back of your head and then cover the second eye and then the first eye again.

- The bandage wrap is even at this point and you no longer need to hold the end.

- As you bring the bandage around the back of your head again, angle the roll upward on the back of your head and then use a downward stroke to cover both eyes.

- On the third layer, angle the bandage downward on the back of your head and sweep the layer upward as you cover your eyes.

- Continue bandaging your head in this manner until you finish the roll.

- When you come to the end of the roll, tuck it into the bandage on the side of your head.

- Keep your eyes closed and allow the eyelids to be soft.

- Place your index fingers under the bandage, starting at the top of your nose, then slide your fingers across your eyelids. This evens out the skin underneath the bandage.

Sometimes we need immediate and effortless relief from our stress. We need Instant Meditation. At times like these, try a few of the following restorative yoga poses and see how quickly your body relaxes and your mind quiets. You will soon feel like a brand-new person.

If you like, you can choose a technique from Quieting the Mind or a meditation from Fix-Its or Going Deeper and use it while you are in one of these poses.

2
Instant Meditation

Lying-Down Postures

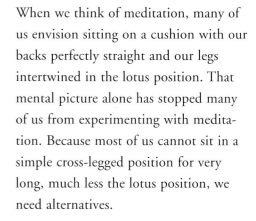

When we think of meditation, many of us envision sitting on a cushion with our backs perfectly straight and our legs intertwined in the lotus position. That mental picture alone has stopped many of us from experimenting with meditation. Because most of us cannot sit in a simple cross-legged position for very long, much less the lotus position, we need alternatives.

So, if you are resisting a sitting meditation practice, lie down in some of these restorative yoga postures. They are designed to relax the body and quiet the mind, making it easier to concentrate on our breath or to focus our thoughts on a specific meditation.

LYING OVER BLANKETS I

Necessary props:
2 to 4 blankets

Optional props:
earplugs, eye cover, 2 more
blankets

In this posture, you will lie over rolled blankets. One blanket will be directly behind your chest, allowing you to do a passive backbend. This allows more oxygen into the lungs and thus into your bloodstream, which naturally makes you feel great. This posture helps relax the body, reducing stress and quieting the mind. It is particularly great to do at the end of a hectic day or when you are not feeling well.

- Fold each blanket in quarters, and then roll it as shown. Place one blanket roll on the floor vertically and the other across it horizontally, a little below center.

- Then test it: Sit in front of the blanket that is vertical, with your hips and lower back at the very edge of the roll. Lie back and adjust the horizontal roll so it falls directly behind your sternum or breastbone.

- You may find that you need another folded blanket or pillow for your head. Test the blanket setup and adjust it until you are perfectly comfortable. For example, depending on the thickness of your blankets, you may find that you want two blankets in each roll.

- When you are sure that the blankets are to your liking, lie down over them.

- Gently close your eyes, use an eye cover and earplugs if you like, and allow your body, mind, and spirit to completely relax. Stay as long as you like; you might even fall asleep.

- When you are ready, come out of the pose by rolling to your right side. Rest there for a few moments and then use your elbow and your hand to bring yourself into a seated position. Be sure to keep your neck soft and to bring your head up last.

LYING OVER BLANKETS II

Necessary props:
2 to 4 blankets

Optional props:
earplugs, an eye cover, 2 more blankets

As in the previous posture, here you will lie over a rolled blanket in a passive backbend. This pose has all the same benefits of the previous pose; the difference is a matter of personal preference.

- Fold one blanket into quarters, and then roll it as shown. Sit several inches in front of the blanket with your back to the horizontally placed blanket. Lie over the roll, with the blanket directly behind your sternum (breastbone).

- If the height of the blanket is not comfortable, make your roll thicker or thinner.

- You may also be more comfortable if you place some folded blankets or a pillow under your head, neck, and shoulders.

- When you have determined that your blanket setup is at its most comfortable, sit in front of it and lie down so the back of your sternum is on the blanket roll.

- Bring the soles of your feet together, and place a rolled blanket or pillow under each thigh so you can easily melt into the posture. If this pose is not 100% comfortable, try Lying Over Blankets I.

- Gently close your eyes. Use an eye cover and earplugs if you like; allow your body, mind, and spirit to completely relax.

- If you like, extend your legs, staying in this position as long as you like.

- When you are ready, roll over to your left side, staying there for a several minutes, using one of the blankets as a pillow for your head. Then roll over to your right side, resting there for a few minutes.

- Come out of the pose by using your elbow and your hand to help you into a seated position. Be sure to keep your neck soft as you sit up, bringing your head up last.

BOOK SUPPORT POSE

Necessary props:
a dictionary-sized book or a yoga block

Optional props:
earplugs, an eye cover, 2 blankets

This pose allows your mind to quiet and also helps relieve headaches and neckaches.

- Place the book or yoga block on the floor.

- Lie on your back with your head on the book or block.

- Bend your knees and place your feet flat on the floor.

- Bring your knees together and place your feet so they are slightly wider than hip distance apart.

- If you are not comfortable, try a thinner book. If that doesn't work, try a thicker one.

- Gently close your eyes, using an eye cover if you like, and focus your inward gaze toward your heart.

- Allow your body and mind to relax naturally. Or try the Exhaling the Mind technique (page 53), which is particularly good to do in this posture.

- Stay in the pose as long as you like. When you are ready, roll over to your right side and rest for a few minutes, supporting your head with the prop, your arm, or a blanket. Using your elbow and your hand, bring yourself into a seated position. Be sure to keep your neck soft as you sit up, bringing your head up last.

CHAIR CORPSE POSE

Necessary props:
chair

Optional props:
earplugs, eye cover, 1 to 4 blankets

This is a popular way to end a yoga session, because it allows the body and mind to become completely quiet. It is called the Corpse Pose because in it we are attempting to simulate death — no thoughts, no worries, no feelings. In the Corpse Pose, we find supreme rest and complete stillness. This pose also helps ease lower back pain.

- Lie on the floor and place your feet and calves on a chair seat.

- Use a blanket or pillow under your head if you like. Use an eye cover and earplugs to help block out distractions.

- Stay in the pose as long as you like.

- When you are ready to come out, bring your knees to your chest and hug them for a few moments. Roll over to your right side and rest there for a few minutes. Using your elbow and your hand, bring yourself into a seated position. Be sure to keep your neck soft as you sit up, bringing your head up last.

PRANAYAMA POSE

Necessary props:
pranayama pillow, 2 to 4 blankets

Optional props:
earplugs, eye cover, extra blankets, neck roll

Pranayama is the yogic discipline of controlled breathing. Pranayama pillows are designed to help open the chest during practice, allowing more oxygen to enter the lungs. The shape of the pillow allows the back muscles to naturally soften and relax. You can lie over the pillow while practicing some of the breathing techniques described in the following sections, or you can allow your body and mind to naturally quiet. These pillows can be purchased through most yoga supply catalogues.

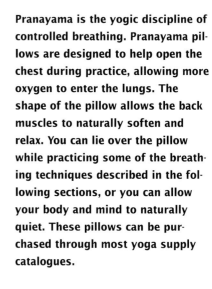

- Place the pranayama pillow vertically on the floor, on some folded blankets, or on your bed.

- Sit in front of the pillow, with the pillow touching your lower back, then lie down on it.

- Place a folded blanket on the top of the pillow for your head, or you can roll a hand towel and place it under your neck. Try both versions and see which is most comfortable for you.

- Lie with your feet extended or with the soles of your feet together.

- Make sure you are completely comfortable in the pose so you can stay in it for 10 to 30 minutes.

- Gently close your eyes, using an eye cover if you like, and focus your inward gaze toward your heart.

- Allow your body and mind to relax naturally, or try the Exhaling the Mind breathing technique (page 53).

If you don't have a pranayama pillow, try using blankets that are folded like an accordion:

- Fold the blanket into quarters.

- Then fold it like an accordion, into even sections, about 6 inches (15 cm) wide.

- Place the folded blanket on the floor, on some other folded blankets, or on your bed.

- Sit in front of the blanket setup with your lower back touching it. Lie down so the accordion-folded blanket is centered on your back.

- Make adjustments for your head and neck using another folded blanket or a neck roll.

LYING IN BED

Necessary props:
bed

Optional props:
earplugs, eye cover, blanket, pillow,
neck roll

If we have no other time to meditate, we can always meditate for a
few minutes when we awaken in the
morning or when we go to sleep at
night. One of the most wonderful
ways to meditate at these times is
to use one of the many Names of
God meditations found in the Going
Deeper section.

Practicing one of the Chakra meditations (pages 62 to 67) also is a
soothing way to fall asleep.

Additionally, I have always found
that an afternoon nap is an alternative to meditation. So if you actually
have time for a nap one weekend
afternoon, use it as an opportunity
to practice your favorite meditation
as you fall asleep.

- Lie down in bed on your back.

- Make sure you are completely comfortable. If you have lower back problems, place a pillow under your knees.

- If your neck bothers you, use your favorite pillow or place a rolled hand towel under your neck.

- Gently close your eyes, covering them if you like, and focus your inward gaze toward your heart.

- Allow your body and mind to relax naturally, falling asleep if that comes naturally. As an alternative, try a breathing technique or a meditation from one of the following sections.

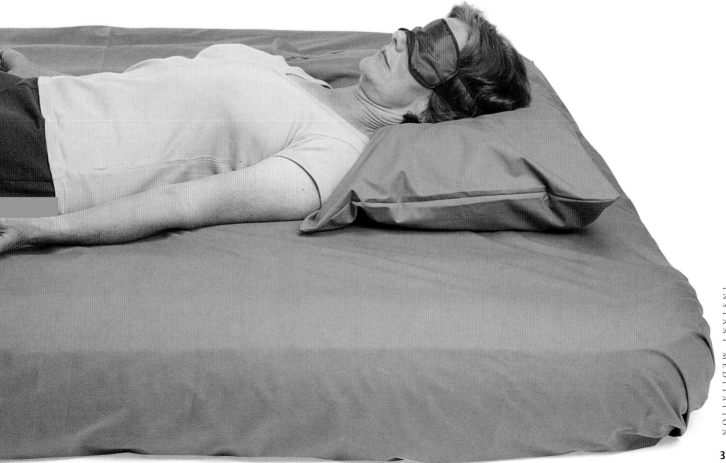

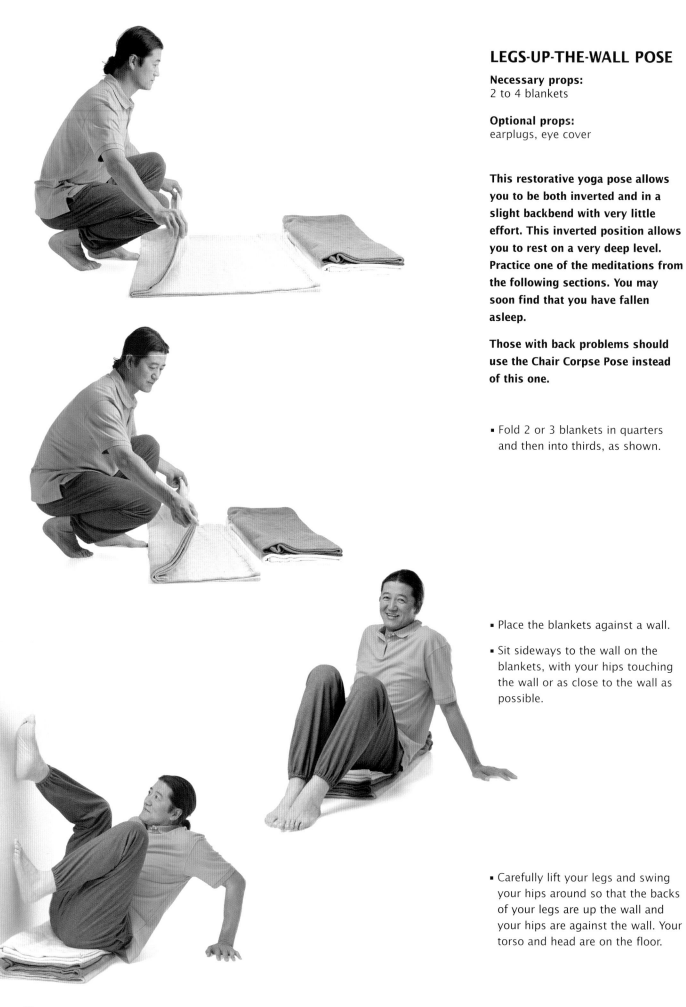

LEGS-UP-THE-WALL POSE

Necessary props:
2 to 4 blankets

Optional props:
earplugs, eye cover

This restorative yoga pose allows you to be both inverted and in a slight backbend with very little effort. This inverted position allows you to rest on a very deep level. Practice one of the meditations from the following sections. You may soon find that you have fallen asleep.

Those with back problems should use the Chair Corpse Pose instead of this one.

- Fold 2 or 3 blankets in quarters and then into thirds, as shown.

- Place the blankets against a wall.

- Sit sideways to the wall on the blankets, with your hips touching the wall or as close to the wall as possible.

- Carefully lift your legs and swing your hips around so that the backs of your legs are up the wall and your hips are against the wall. Your torso and head are on the floor.

- If your neck is uncomfortable, fold and place another blanket under your head.

- Gently close your eyes, covering them if you like, and focus your inward gaze toward your heart.

- Allow your body and mind to relax naturally.

- Lie in this position as long as you like. If your legs get tired, bend your knees without adjusting the rest of your pose.

- When you are ready to come out of the pose, slide your hips off the blankets toward your head. Roll to your right side, and rest there for a few minutes before sitting up.

Note: If your shoulders or arms are not completely comfortable, fold 2 blankets and place one under each arm, from the shoulder to the hand.

Seated Postures

As your stress starts to release through the various restorative poses that you are now practicing, you may want to try more formal or traditional meditation postures. Some Eastern meditation traditions advise that the spine should be perfectly straight while meditating. This allows the kundalini energy, which is considered the life force located at the base of the spine, to travel upward toward the head. As a result, the life force is distributed throughout the body. If you find yourself slumping, try lifting your sternum (breastbone) and lifting your lower back muscles and your lower abdominal muscles. Keep your shoulders relaxed. If you sit for meditation, always lie down afterwards for at least 5 minutes to allow yourself the time to slowly reenter the world.

SITTING IN A CHAIR

Sitting in a chair is the easiest seated meditation posture, because sitting in a chair is something we do every day.

Necessary props:
sturdy chair

Optional props:
earplugs, eye cover

- Sit comfortably in the chair.

- Lift your lower back and abdominal muscles.

- Make sure your torso is aligned with your hips.

- Lift your sternum (breastbone). When you lift your sternum, do not lift your shoulders toward your ears. The shoulders are slightly back, the upper back is straight, and the shoulders are relaxed.

- Keep your head aligned with your spine, not tilting forward, backward, or to either side. Soften your throat, neck, and face.

- Place the backs of your hands on your thighs, and, if you like, hold your hands in one of the mudras described in the *Common Terms* section.

- Gently close your eyes and focus your inward gaze toward your heart.

- Focus on your breath or choose a meditation from one of the following sections.

HERO'S POSE

Necessary props:
thick books or yoga blocks

Optional props:
blanket, earplugs, eye cover

This seated posture naturally helps keep the spine straight, so your back may be more comfortable in this pose than in other seated poses. However, if you have very tight hips, you may not find it comfortable and may need to adjust the height of the block by adding another block or a folded blanket.

As you become more comfortable in this pose and gain flexibility in your hips, you will be able to sit on lower and lower props. Eventually, you may be comfortable sitting on the floor.

This pose also helps alleviate knee problems, increases flexibility in the knees and hips, improves circulation, and reduces varicose veins.

- Place a very thick book or a yoga block on the floor.

- Kneel, with your knees hip-distance apart, in front of the book or block.

- Roll your calves outward as you move into the seated position. Release your calves at the last moment possible as you sit on the block.

- If your knees are uncomfortable, add another book or block. If you can't get comfortable, try a different pose.

- If your ankles are unhappy, roll up two face towels and place one under each ankle.

- Lift your lower back muscles and lower abdominal muscles.

- Make sure your torso is aligned with your hips.

- Lift your sternum (breastbone). When you lift your sternum, do not lift your shoulders toward your ears. The shoulders are back, the upper back is straight, and the shoulders are relaxed.

- Keep your head aligned with your spine — not tilting forward, backward, or to either side. Soften your throat, neck, and face.

- Place the backs of your hands on your thighs, and, if you like, use one of the mudras described on pages 17 to 18.

- Gently close your eyes and allow your inward gaze to be toward your heart.

- Start by sitting for 3 to 4 minutes. Over time, you can stay in this seated posture for longer and longer periods.

- Focus on your breath or use a meditation from one of the following sections.

SUPER-SIMPLE CROSS-LEGGED POSTURE

Necessary props:
3 or 4 blankets, 2 washcloths,
2 pillows

In this seated posture, the height and the evenness of the folded blankets put less stress on the lower back than sitting on the floor or on uneven pillows or cushions.

When I started meditating, I had a tremendous amount of back and knee pain from recent injuries. All of the variations shown here make you more comfortable if you have similar aches and pains.

- Fold 2 blankets in quarters and then into thirds.

- Place one blanket on top of the other.

- Sit on the blankets in a simple cross-legged position.

- Pad each thigh with a folded or rolled blanket or pillow to give your thighs support. This way, the inner thighs and knees can more easily relax.

- Place the backs of your hands on your thighs, and, if you like, use one of the mudras described on page 17 or 18.

- Lift your lower back muscles, your lower abdominal muscles, and your sternum. When you lift your sternum, do not lift your shoulders toward your ears. The shoulders are back, the upper back is straight, and the shoulders are relaxed.

- Make sure your torso is aligned with your hips.

- Keep your head aligned with your spine, not tilting forward, backward, or to either side. Soften your throat, neck, and face.

- Gently close your eyes and allow your inward gaze to be toward your heart.

- Focus on your breath or choose a meditation from one of the following sections.

- If your knees get stiff, relieve the discomfort by extending the legs. Try to make the act of extending your legs a meditation by being fully conscious and aware of your movement.

- If you feel that you need some back support, try sitting against a wall or place a pillow between your back and the wall.

- Another suggestion for knee pain: try placing rolled hand towels on the insides of your knees, as shown, and cross your legs again.

THE ZAZEN BENCH POSTURE

Necessary props:
zazen bench

Optional props:
earplugs, eye cover

Zazen is a seated meditation used in Zen Buddhism. Zazen benches are low benches available through meditation-supplies catalogues. Sitting on a zazen bench is very similar to sitting in Hero's Pose in that the back naturally straightens. The difference is that the zazen bench is higher than yoga blocks or dictionaries, making the pose even easier for those with tight hips or knees.

- Kneel in front of the bench with your calves underneath it.

- Roll your calves outward and sit back, releasing your calves at the last possible moment possible prior to sitting.

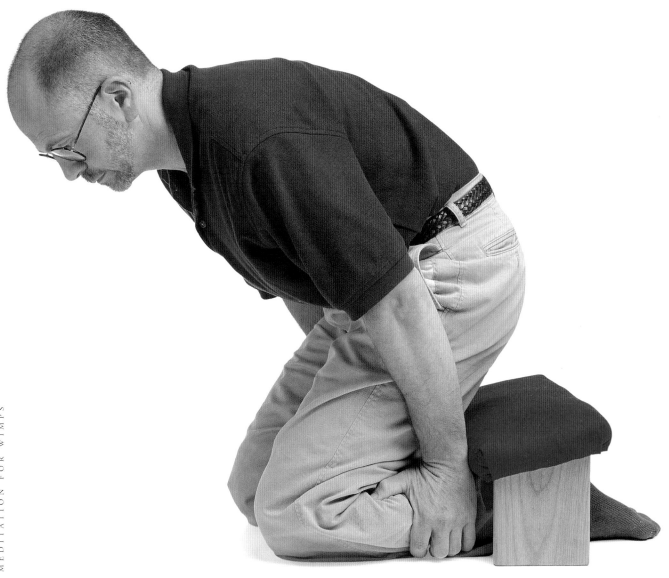

- Lift your lower back muscles, your lower abdominal muscles, and your sternum. When you lift your sternum, do not lift your shoulders toward your ears. The shoulders are back, the upper back is straight, and the shoulders are relaxed.

- Make sure your torso is aligned with your hips.

- Keep your head aligned with your spine — not tilting forward, backward, or to either side. Soften your throat, neck, and face.

- Place the backs of your hands on your thighs, and, if you like, use one of the mudras described on pages 17 to 18.

- Gently close your eyes and allow your inward gaze to be toward your heart.

- Focus on your breath, or choose a meditation from one of the following sections.

Alternative Meditation Postures

STANDING MEDITATION: TADASANA

Tadasana (Mountain Pose) is a yogic standing posture. When we stand correctly, we feel as strong as a mountain, grounded to the earth and soaring toward the heavens. Try this pose at home so you can learn how to stand in this powerful way. Then, whenever you are in line at the grocery store or the bank, or any other place you have to stand and wait, you can practice it and feel the strength of your own power while performing this simple standing meditation.

- If you are a beginner, stand with your feet slightly separated and parallel to each other. As you gain proficiency in this pose, stand with your toes touching and your heels slightly separated.

- Feel that your weight is evenly distributed on your feet so that you are not putting more weight on the balls of your feet or on the heels.

- Lift your quadriceps (the muscles on the front of the thighs) toward your hips. This is a lifting or a contracting of the muscles, not a locking of the knees.

- Lift your lower back muscles and lower tummy muscles up and slightly in toward each other.

- Lift your sternum (breastbone). When you lift your sternum, do not lift your shoulders toward your ears. The shoulders are slightly back, the upper back is straight, and the shoulders are relaxed.

Meditation is THE comfort in life.

— SRI SRI RAVI SHANKAR

- Make sure that your torso is completely aligned with your hips, not leaning forward or backward.

- Keep your head aligned with your spine, not tilting forward, backward, or to either side. Soften your throat, neck, and face.

- As you stand in Tadasana, focus on the position of your body. Feel the energy in your feet and legs, which ground you to earth. Be aware of the center of your body: the base of your spine and pelvic area. In yoga, it is believed that all of the body's energy comes from the base of your spine. Feel the energy that comes from your center.

WALKING MEDITATION

Walking meditation serves many purposes. For those who regularly practice sitting meditation, particularly for long periods of time, walking meditation helps reenergize the body and relieves fatigue and stiffness. For those who are very active and have a difficult time sitting or lying down to meditate, walking meditation helps develop mindfulness, a practice that helps us become aware and present in each moment.

Walking meditation can be practiced indoors or outdoors. In either case, mark off a certain area: 10, 20, or 50 feet (3, 6, or 15 metres). If you are walking indoors, I suggest you walk without shoes.

- Stand in Tadasana (see page 46) at the start of your marked-off area.

- Consciously move one foot forward, aware of how your foot touches the ground. Feel the heel, middle of the foot, ball of the foot, and the toes as they touch the ground. Be aware of how your leg muscles contract.

- Move the second foot forward with the same amount of attentiveness.

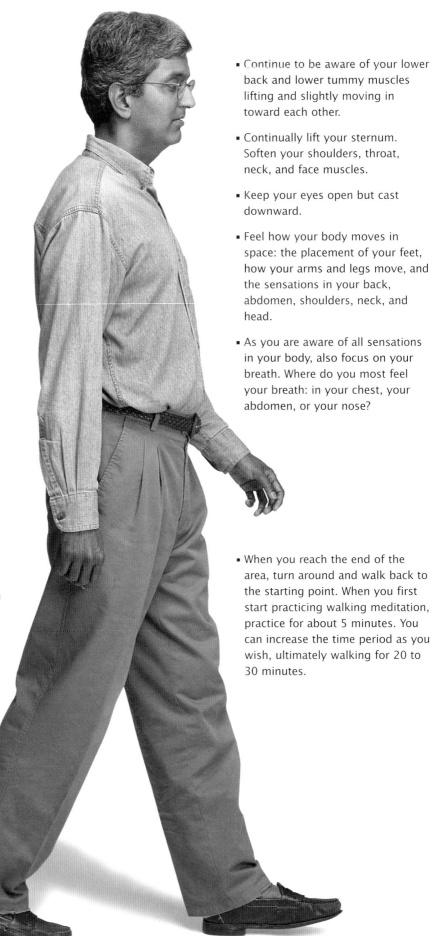

- Continue to be aware of your lower back and lower tummy muscles lifting and slightly moving in toward each other.

- Continually lift your sternum. Soften your shoulders, throat, neck, and face muscles.

- Keep your eyes open but cast downward.

- Feel how your body moves in space: the placement of your feet, how your arms and legs move, and the sensations in your back, abdomen, shoulders, neck, and head.

- As you are aware of all sensations in your body, also focus on your breath. Where do you most feel your breath: in your chest, your abdomen, or your nose?

- When you reach the end of the area, turn around and walk back to the starting point. When you first start practicing walking meditation, practice for about 5 minutes. You can increase the time period as you wish, ultimately walking for 20 to 30 minutes.

FOREHEAD-TO-CHAIR TECHNIQUE

Necessary props:
chair

Optional props:
earplugs, Ace bandage eye cover, blanket, dictionary-sized book, wooden yoga block, blanket

Although this is not a traditional meditation posture, there are few techniques I know that quiet a chattering mind as quickly as this one does. Try it when you feel particularly stressed and see how quickly your body and mind become calm and quiet.

- Sit in comfortable position (with legs at a wide angle, straight out, or cross-legged) in front of a chair.

- Use earplugs and an Ace bandage eye cover if you like.

- Place your hands on the chair seat as shown.

- Place your forehead on the chair seat or on your hands, which are on the chair seat.

- Be sure to rest the area between your eyebrows on the chair.

- Breathe deep into your lower back. Allow each exhalation to soften your body and quiet your mind.

- If your flexibility is limited and this is not comfortable, place a book or folded blanket on the chair seat and then place your forehead on that prop.

- At the office, seated at your desk, place your hands on a book on your desk and rest your forehead on them. You must be 100% comfortable in this pose. If not, try another posture.

- If you are more flexible, try placing your forehead on a yoga block instead of a chair.

Without any prompting, our minds think. We brood over the past or anxiously contemplate the future. Often we don't even know where the thoughts come from or how or why they enter our head. Sometimes we wonder, "Who is thinking this stuff?"

Quieting our mind is the supreme vacation, the ultimate get away from it all. When we think we need to get off the merry-go-round of life, what we really need to do is quiet our minds.

All of the spiritual traditions encourage us to empty our minds, contending that a silent mind is an experience of God, our Buddha nature, or the Tao. This section includes several breathing techniques for quieting the mind and one other, very surprising method. These techniques can be used as meditations or they can be used to prepare for meditation.

3

Quieting the Mind

Empty your mind of all thoughts,

let your heart be at peace.

— LAO TZU

Watching the Breath

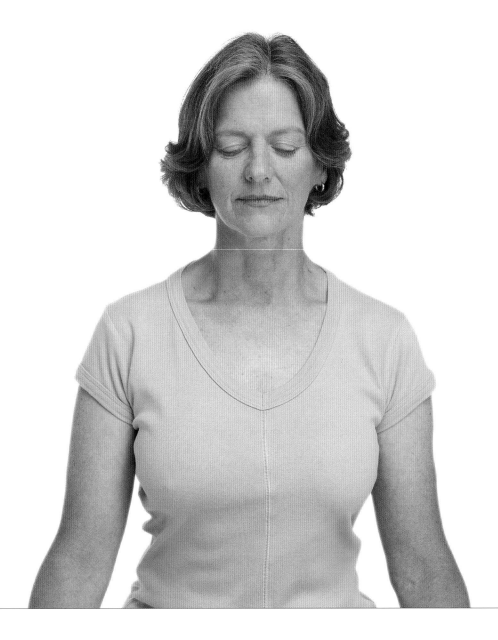

SEATED BREATH-WATCHING MEDITATION

Sitting and watching the breath is a well-known meditation technique. Naturally, the mind wanders. But each time we become aware of our thoughts, we gently bring our attention back to the breath. By doing so, we become more aware of our thoughts and learn that we don't have to attach any significance to those thoughts. They are just thoughts. As we do this, the mind becomes more and more tranquil.

- Sit or lie down in your favorite meditation posture.

- To prepare, go through the General Relaxation routine found on pages 20 to 22.

- At the end of that relaxation period, start to follow your breath. Don't try to control it, just watch it.

- You can focus on your breath at the tip of the nose, as it flows in and out. Or you can place your attention on the rise and fall of your abdomen.

- Each time you become aware of your thoughts, gently bring your attention back to your breath.

- Initially, practice this meditation for 3 or 4 minutes. As you progress, increase the time a minute or two longer than your previous meditation. Eventually, practice this breathing meditation for 20 to 30 minutes.

Controlling the Breath

Techniques to control the breath are rooted in traditional Hindu yoga and meditation practices. As a whole, the practice is called *pranayama.* It is defined as the rhythmic control of the breath. Here are some simple ways to practice pranayama.

EXHALING THE MIND

This is a terrific meditation that allows our minds to become silent quickly. Many of my students have told me that through this meditation they have instantly and effortlessly let go of persistent worries. If you like, you can start this meditation by going through the General Relaxation found on pages 20 to 22.

Inhaling 1, 2, 3.
Exhaling 1, 2, 3, 4, 5, 6.

- Sit or lie down in your favorite meditation posture.

- Gently close your eyes and focus your inward gaze toward your heart.

- Make the intention that you are practicing this meditation to quiet your mind.

- Focus on your breath for a minute or two to relax your body and quiet your mind.

- Now you are ready to alter the exhalation. Take normal inhalations and long, slow, smooth exhalations. You can practice this breath by mentally counting:

- Count your breaths for a few rounds until you get the knack of it. Once you feel comfortable with the breath, let go of the counting.

- Focus on normal inhalations, followed by long, slow, smooth exhalations.

- With each exhalation, allow all your thoughts to be released through the nose. On your exhalation, imagine that all thoughts, all worries, and all concerns flow out of your mind, through your nostrils, and out of your body.

- As you exhale your thoughts, begin to imagine that the mind itself is actually being exhaled. Take nor-

mal inhalations and long, slow, smooth exhalations, exhaling the mind.

- Your face will continue to soften and your eyes and eyelids will become more and more relaxed.

- Your mind will continue to quiet more and more as you exhale your thoughts and your mind.

- Initially practice this meditation for 3 or 4 minutes. As you progress, increase the time at each session a minute or two more than your previous meditation. Eventually, practice this breathing technique for 20 to 30 minutes at a time.

ALTERNATE-NOSTRIL BREATHING

Before trying this technique, take a few moments to understand the necessary hand movements. This practice is traditionally done with the right hand. You will use the thumb to close the right nostril and, alternately, the pinky and ring finger to close the left nostril. The forefinger and middle finger should be folded into the palm. The ring finger and pinky are slightly bent.

- To start practicing, place the ring and pinky fingers on the left nostril, close to the bottom of the nose. Gently close the left nostril with the pinky and the ring finger and slowly inhale through the right nostril.

- To exhale, close the right nostril with the thumb, and slowly exhale through the now opened left nostril.

- Then slowly inhale through the left nostril, close off the left nostril, and slowly exhale through the now opened right nostril.

Now that you have learned the technique, get ready for the full practice of alternate-nostril breathing.

- Sit in your favorite meditation posture.

- Tilt your head slightly forward so the chin is near the chest.

- Gently close your eyes, releasing all tension from the eyes, as though you are quietly withdrawing from the world.

- Carefully close your left nostril with your pinky and ring finger.

- Slowly inhale through the right nostril and then gently release the left nostril and close the right one with your thumb.

- Slowly and fully exhale through the left nostril.

- Keeping the left nostril open, slowly inhale, close the left nostril, and then slowly and fully exhale through the now opened right nostril.

- Slowly inhale though the right nostril, close it, open the left nostril, and exhale.

- Proceed with this breathing exercise for about 2 minutes; then resume normal breathing for 2 minutes.

- Start the alternate-nostril breathing again, continuing for 2 minutes.

- Resume normal breathing and focus on a favorite meditation, or lie down and rest for a few minutes.

- As you progress, you will no longer need the periods of normal breathing. You can then increase the periods of the alternate-nostril breathing to 5 to 10 minutes.

THE LALALA MEDITATION

I learned this meditation from the Hindu master Sri Sri Ravi Shankar, founder of the Art of Living Foundation. You will be delightfully surprised with the results.

- Sit in your favorite meditation posture.

- Gently close your eyes and focus your inward gaze toward your heart.

- Start repeating *LA LA LA* aloud.

LA LA LA LA LA LA LA LA LA LA LA

LA LA LA LA LA LA LA LA LA LA LA

LA LA LA LA LA LA LA LA LA LA LA

LA LA LA LA LA LA LA LA LA LA LA

LA LA LA LA LA LA LA LA LA LA LA

- After about 2 minutes, change the tone of your voice and notice if there are any changes in how you feel.

- Try going faster and slower. Notice the changes.

- Repeat *LA LA LA* for 5 to 10 minutes. Then simply lie down and see how you feel!

LA is a primordial human sound. In other words, LA is a fundamental, original sound, which all babies make without ever being taught. It is already within us. By practicing this meditation, we bring ourselves back to our primordial self, our divine self, the part of us that is one with God, one with Cosmic Consciousness.

BASTRIKA

Bastrika is Sanskrit for "bellows," a device that produces a stream of air through a narrow tube when it is pressed together. Bellows are used in furnaces and pipe organs. In this technique, air is forcefully inhaled and exhaled, similar to the blasting of air through a furnace. Although Bastrika is a very active breathing technique, it has a very calming effect on the mind. A seated position is preferred, but you can also do this standing.

- Sit in your favorite meditation posture.

- Gently close your eyes and focus your inward gaze toward your heart.

- Focus on your breath for a minute or two to relax your body and quiet your mind.

- Close your hands into fists and place your fists at the sides of your shoulders. The upper arms are on the sides of the chest.

- Take a normal inhalation and a normal exhalation.

- Extend your hands over your head, taking a large, forceful inhalation and opening your palms.

- Forcefully exhale, closing your hands and bringing your arms back to their starting position.

- Repeat this breathing pattern 12 to 15 times. Then sit quietly for 2 to 3 minutes with your eyes closed.

- Perform two more sets of 12 to 15 rounds, resting for a few minutes between them.

- When you have finished, practice one of your favorite meditations or lie down to rest for a few minutes.

While meditation is rooted in ancient spiritual and religious traditions, secular meditations can help us address the challenges and problems we face in our everyday lives. The word meditate *comes from the Latin word* mederi, *which means "to remedy." This chapter includes meditations that remedy — or fix — our everyday problems.*

I have learned all of these meditations from friends, books, or meditation masters. Some are derived from specific spiritual traditions but have been secularized so they can be used by everyone. All of these meditations work. I can say that because I have lived these meditations — and their results. I use them repeatedly when I have a specific challenge or when I simply need to soothe my soul. Because these meditations have helped me, I can wholeheartedly prescribe them to you as remedies for difficulties you might encounter.

4

Fix-Its

Making Everything Better

If only there were a magic potion to relieve all of our problems! Or a salve to heal both our physical and emotional pain. While there is no magic potion or salve, we do have meditation. Meditation makes us feel better, both in the short run and in the long run. So next time you crave a magic potion, try the meditations in this section, because they really do make everything better.

THE LOVING-KINDNESS MEDITATION

If there is a fast track to alleviating our own suffering and to helping others ease their pain, The Loving-Kindness Meditation is it. It comes from the Buddhist tradition.

- Sit or lie down in your favorite meditation posture.

- Gently close your eyes and focus your inward gaze toward your heart.

- Make the intention that you are practicing this meditation to increase your inner peace, to heal yourself, or to expand your inner joy.

- Focus on your breath for a minute or two to relax your body and quiet your mind.

- When you are ready, on your inhalation, silently repeat:

May I be free from suffering.

- On your exhalation, silently repeat:

May I be at peace.

- Allow yourself to truly feel these good wishes for yourself.

- Depending on your situation, you might want to change the meditation a little:

May I be free from suffering.
May I be healed.

or

May I be free from suffering.
May I be full of joy.

During the same meditation session or on another day, try the Loving-Kindness Meditation to direct kind thoughts to others who are in pain, either physically or emotionally. Visualize a friend, loved one, or a group of people who are suffering while you practice one of these meditations for them.

May you be free from suffering.
May you be at peace.

or

May you be free from suffering.
May you be full of joy.

or

May you be free from suffering.
May you be healed.

VARIATIONS OF THE LOVING-KINDNESS MEDITATION

There are many ways you can use this meditation. When you or a friend have a particular problem, you can devise a meditation for that specific concern. For example, if you are having a problem with self-confidence and self-esteem, you can meditate in this way:

May I be full of confidence.
May I enjoy great self-esteem.

- If your friend is having a problem with self-confidence, change the meditation to:

May you be full of confidence.
May you enjoy great self-esteem.

- If you are trying to increase your understanding of others, try this version:

May I be loving, kind, and understanding of all people *(or name a specific person).*

- If you are in the midst of turmoil about making an important decision, a suggested variation is:

May I be free from suffering.
May I make wise decisions.

THE TRADITIONAL BUDDHIST VERSION OF THE LOVING-KINDNESS MEDITATION

The Loving-Kindness Meditation comes from the Buddhist tradition, but for beginning meditators, the traditional Buddhist version can seem a little awkward. In Buddhism, it is believed that the root of suffering is our attachment to our desires and that the root of happiness is the complete acceptance of everything in our lives. As you progress in your meditation practice, you may want to practice this traditional meditation.

May I be free from suffering and the root of suffering.

May I enjoy happiness and the root of happiness.

- If you are meditating for another person, say:

May you be free from suffering and the root of suffering.

May you enjoy happiness and the root of happiness.

Chakra Meditations

The following meditations soothe the body, mind, and spirit. I like to do these meditations when I take an afternoon nap or as I go to sleep at night. Their origin is in Kundalini yoga.

Chakra is a Sanskrit word that means "wheel" or "ring." Chakras are energy centers located along the spine. These centers absorb vibrations from within our bodies and from the world around us and radiate that energy throughout the body. When our chakras are balanced, we are happy in all aspects of our lives. When they are out of balance, our body, mind, and spirit are out of equilibrium. Through modern physiology, we know that the seven chakras correspond exactly to the seven main nerve ganglia which arise from the spinal cord. No wonder they are so important.

Each chakra is said to have a distinct meaning. Specific colors and mantras are associated with each chakra. Each chakra is envisioned as a lotus. This chart lists the chakra locations, meanings, and colors.

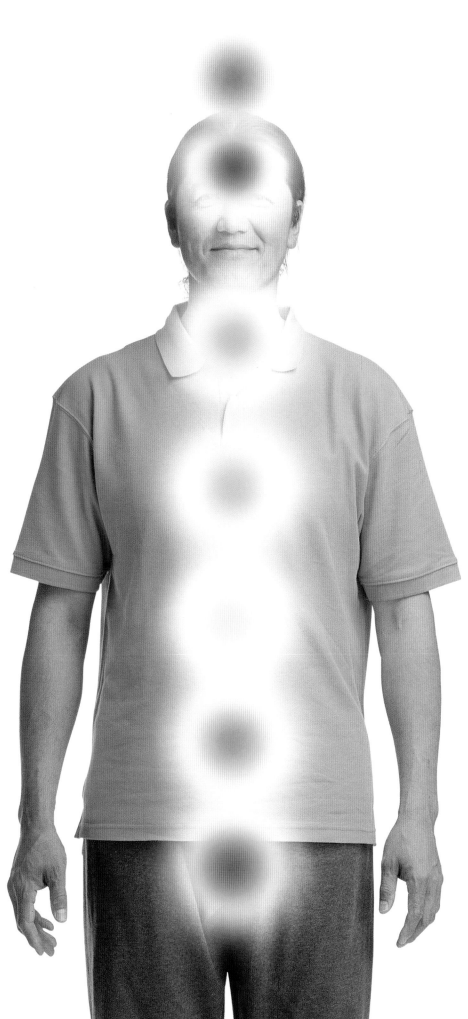

Seventh Chakra: The Crown Chakra
- Location: The crown of the head
- Meaning: Spiritual connection and belief system
- Color: Violet

Sixth Chakra: The Third Eye
- Location: Center of the eyebrows
- Meaning: Wisdom
- Color: Indigo

Fifth Chakra: The Throat Chakra
- Location: Center of the throat
- Meaning: Communication and self-expression
- Color: Light blue

Fourth Chakra: The Heart Chakra
- Location: The heart area
- Meaning: Love and relationships
- Color: Green

Third Chakra: The Solar Plexus
- Location: The solar plexus
- Meaning: Will power and motivation
- Color: Yellow

Second Chakra: The Creative Chakra
- Location: About 2 inches (5 cm) below the navel
- Meaning: Creativity and pleasure
- Color: Orange

First Chakra: The Base Chakra
- Location: Base of the spine
- Meaning: Grounding and survival
- Color: Red

The next two meditations involve the body's 7 chakras.

THE WHITE LIGHT MEDITATION

In every heart Thou art hidden;

In every heart burns Thy light.

> — GURU NANAK

O Lord, make light grow within me and give me light and

illuminate me.

> — MUHAMMAD

And when the soul reaches its source, it cleaves to the

celestial light from which it derives and the two become one.

> — GERSHOM SCHOLEM

For God, who commanded the light to shine out of

darkness, hath shined in our hearts, to give the light of

the knowledge of the glory of God in the face of Jesus

Christ.

> — ST. PAUL

Gently eliminating all obstacles to his own understanding,

he constantly maintains his unconditional sincerity. His

humility, perseverance, and adaptability evoke the

response of the universe and fill him with divine light.

> — LAO TZU

If, while you're walking, standing, sitting, or lying in a

quiet grove, you see a light, regardless of whether it's

bright or dim, don't tell others and don't focus on it. It's

the light of your own nature.

> — BODHIDHARMA

As you can see from the quotes, all spiritual traditions believe that God manifests as light. In this meditation, the white light is the Divine white light, the light of Universal Consciousness, the spark of the Divine within you.

This meditation is extremely relaxing. It calms the nervous system on a very deep level. If you do it while lying down, you may fall asleep before finishing, which is great.

- Sit or lie down in a comfortable meditation posture.

- Gently close your eyes and focus your inward gaze toward your heart.

- Focus your attention on your breath for a minute or two to relax your body and quiet your mind.

- Imagine a radiant, white light above you and surrounding you. The light is peaceful, calm, warm, and healing.

- Visualize this light coming into the crown of your head. The light completely fills your head.

- Then imagine this beautiful white light coming into the place between your eyebrows. Allow the light to permeate your head and your face, softening all of your facial muscles.

- Next, bring the white light into the middle of your throat, allowing it to pervade your entire throat and neck. Feel how the tension in your neck and throat releases.

- Then, focusing on your heart, bring the white light into your heart center, allowing your whole chest — the front, the back, and the sides of the chest — to be filled with this white light.

- Concentrating on your solar plexus, bring the light in, allowing that area, both front and back, to soften and relax.

- Then allow the light to enter your body about 2 inches (5 cm) below your navel, letting the light permeate that area of your body. Feel the warm sensation of the light.

- Finally, bring the white light into the area at the very base of your spine, receiving the light into the lower back and hips, feeling all tension release.

- Visualize and feel the white light from the very top of your head to the very base of your spine, through the head, neck, shoulders, and torso. Disperse the light into your arms and hands and then into your legs and feet. Your entire body is filled with white light.

- Once you are finished, if you are in a reclining posture, stay there for several minutes. If you are seated, lie down until you feel restored.

- Feel the transformative power of the light within you.

SUGGESTED VARIATIONS: Each chakra is associated with its own color (see the chakra chart). Instead of using white light, use the color that corresponds to each individual chakra.

Eliminate the cause, the very root of negativity. Instead of rubbing the mind with a positive thought, go deep into yourself through the breath and meditation — they clean the system.

— SRI SRI RAVI SHANKAR

BREATHING INTO EACH CHAKRA

Choose a seated or lying-down meditation posture. If you do this meditation lying down, there is a good chance you will fall asleep before you are finished. If that happens, go with it. This meditation relaxes the nervous system on a very deep level. If you choose to practice this meditation while seated, schedule your time so you can rest or nap afterward.

When you first start practicing this meditation, be sure to focus your breathing on each chakra for 1 to 2 minutes. After you have explored this meditation several times, you can increase the time you spend breathing into each chakra to 4 to 5 minutes. If necessary, prior to practicing this meditation, refer to the chakra chart.

- Sit or lie down in your favorite meditation posture.

- Gently close your eyes and focus your inward gaze toward your heart.

- Focus your attention on your breath for a minute or two to relax your body and quiet your mind.

- Direct your breath to the chakra at the base of your spine. Imagine that your breath is entering and leaving the body in that place instead of through the nose. Completely focus the breath in that area. Inhale at the base of your spine, exhale from the base of your spine.

- Then move up to the second chakra, which is located about 2 inches (5 cm) below your navel, following the same technique. Breathe into the second chakra. Experience your breath in both the front and the back of the body, appreciating the relaxation that comes into the lower back and abdomen.

- Then, the third chakra. Feel the breath at your solar plexus. Inhale and exhale at the solar plexus. Sense the breath at the front and the back of the body.

- The fourth chakra. Focus your attention on your heart center. Inhale and exhale at the heart center, conscious of the breath and the energy at your heart.

- Move to the throat chakra, the fifth chakra. Breathe in and out at the throat. Feel the relaxation that comes into both the throat and the neck.

- The sixth chakra is at the third eye. Direct the breath to the center of your eyebrows: inhale and exhale from the center of your eyebrows.

- After a few minutes, move to the seventh chakra, the crown chakra, breathing in and out through the top of your head. Allowing your breath to penetrate the crown of your head. Inhale and exhale through the top of your head. Continue for several minutes.

- Once you are finished, if you are in a reclining posture, stay there and rest. If you are seated, lie down until you feel restored.

Overcoming Obstacles

We all face obstacles, internal and external: Anger, fear, sadness, envy, pride, feelings of inadequacy. The judgment of others, barriers to promotions at work, prejudice from others. Whatever their source, all obstacles reduce our inner peace and harmony. Whatever obstacles you are facing, try some of the following meditations and watch the obstacles dissolve within the goodness of your own heart.

Overcoming Anger

We all know that anger is a double-edged sword. When we release our rage on someone, we feel better for a bit, because anger gives us tremendous power. Our anger is gone, but we have unloaded it on someone else, who then becomes angry or upset. After our short-lived euphoria, we regret our behavior, and now have another obstacle to deal with.

The techniques and meditations given here can be practiced when you are in the throes of anger or to help you release deep-seated anger.

Should one person ignorantly do wrong

And another ignorantly become angry (with him)

Who would be at fault?

And who would be without fault?

— SHANTIDEVA

CALMING ANGER MEDITATION

This meditation is recommended by Thich Nhat Hahn, a Vietnamese Buddhist monk who was nominated for the Nobel Peace Prize by Dr. Martin Luther King for his peace efforts during the Vietnam war. Thich Nhat Hahn and his fellow monks were often the target of ridicule and aggression. The following meditation is based on the technique he taught his fellow monks to practice when they became angry.

- Sit or lie down in your favorite meditation posture.
- Gently close your eyes and focus your inward gaze toward your heart.
- Make the intention that your are practicing this meditation to calm your anger as quickly as possible.
- Silently repeat the meditation, synchronizing the breath appropriately:

Inhaling I calm my anger.
Exhaling I calm my anger.

- Continue until you truly feel calm.

A word spoken in anger is the sharpest sword.

— BUDDHA

Behind anger is a desire. It's a desire that is the cause of anger. Unless you root out the desire, you can never be devoid of anger.

— SRI SRI RAVI SHANKAR

MANTRA WALK

Here is a more active solution to your anger.

- As you feel your anger rising, quickly remove yourself from the situation.

- Go take a walk. Keep a brisk pace. As you walk, repeat the following mantra:

I am patience.
I am patience.
I am patience.

THE "HMMMPH" TECHNIQUE

This is a technique taught by people at the Art of Living Foundation. It quickly releases anger without making someone else a target for that anger.

- This meditation can be practiced sitting or standing, with your eyes open or closed.

- Place your right hand on your solar plexus.

- Take a deep inhalation. Exhale forcefully with your mouth closed and make the "Hmmmph" sound, focusing the sound at your solar plexus.

- Do this 5 or 6 times. Relax for a minute or two. If you continue to feel some anger, repeat another 5 or 6 times. Relax and feel the change in your body and in your mood.

- You can use the "Hmmmph" Technique almost anywhere: in your office with the door closed, in a restroom stall, in a phone booth.

Overcoming Indecision

Life often presents us with very difficult choices, causing confusion and indecision. If the choice were between "good" and "bad," we would have no problem. But the choices are often between "bad" and "worse." Next time you are having a difficult time making up your mind, try the following meditation.

OVERCOMING INDECISION MEDITATION

- Sit or lie down in your favorite meditation posture.

- Gently close your eyes and focus your inward gaze toward your heart.

- Make the intention that you are doing this meditation practice to help you make a decision about the issue that is currently concerning you.

- Focus on your breath for a minute or two to relax your body and quiet your mind.

- Start to focus on your heart, feeling its energy. Feel your chest rise and fall as you breathe. Begin to think about your current situation.

- As a possible solution presents itself, take it into your heart. Physically sense how this solution feels. Does your heart feel calm and serene? Does the pace of your heartbeat speed up? Do you feel an uncomfortable fluttering in your heart center? Do you feel fearful? Do you feel excited? Do you feel peaceful or uncomfortable? Happy or sad?

- Then take the next solution into your heart. Again feel the physical sensations associated with this option. You may also feel sensations in your stomach.

- The negative sensations you feel probably indicate a "no" or "not yet" to that particular option. The alternatives that bring feelings of peace and tranquility usually indicate "yes."

- Continue the practice until you have examined each possibility within your heart. Your body, heart, and mind will feel the clarity when you have found the right solution.

Overcoming Fear and Other Obstacles

Most of life is uncertain. We often become uncomfortable, anxious, or fearful about our present circumstances or possible future events. When you find yourself in this situation, the following meditation will help calm your fears.

OVERCOMING FEAR MEDITATION

- Sit or lie down in your favorite meditation posture.

- Gently close your eyes and focus your inward gaze toward your heart.

- Make the intention that you are practicing this meditation to help ease your anxiety about the uncertainty in your life.

- Focus on your breath for a minute or two to relax your body and quiet your mind.

- On the inhalation silently repeat:

May I be safe and secure.

- On the exhalation, silently repeat:

May I be safe and secure.

- Continue the meditation as long as you like.

In addition to doing this as a formal meditation, you can repeat these phrases as you are going to sleep, as you do your manual chores, while walking, while waiting in line, etc.

BLACK SMOKE/WHITE SMOKE MEDITATION

Sometimes we cannot overcome our obstacles until we fully embrace them. Of course, we don't want to fully embrace our obstacles because it is often just too painful. This meditation allows us to face our obstacles, release them, and find solutions within the goodness of our own hearts. My friend David Bierman taught me this meditation many years ago. I have used it to overcome a wide variety of obstacles.

- Sit or lie down in your favorite meditation posture.

- Gently close your eyes and focus your inward gaze toward your heart.

- Focusing on your heart, remind yourself of all the goodness that resides within. Allow yourself to truly feel your goodness, kindness, compassion, understanding, serenity, humor, integrity, generosity, patience, joy, and love.

- Now imagine an obstacle that is currently bothering you. Visualize that difficulty as a ball of black smoke above your head. Really focus on this obstacle and, in your mind's eye, truly see this obstacle as black smoke.

- Start to inhale the black smoke, bringing that obstacle into your body and into your consciousness. Allow yourself to be fully engaged. Bringing it into your being allows you to completely experience the obstacle.

- Then imagine that this obstacle is being purified in your heart. Knowing that the obstacle is transformed, visualize that you are exhaling the solution, the purification of the problem, as white smoke.

- Continue the process, inhaling the problem or obstacle as black smoke and exhaling the solution as white smoke.

- Start with 5 to 10 minutes or meditate until you feel complete for the session. Then rest quietly for a few minutes, once again focusing on your own inherent goodness.

From Blues to Bliss

Everyone experiences the blues. Jazz musicians have glamorized the blues, but when we are in the throes of hard times, all we want is to get out. Next time you find yourself feeling down, try the following meditations to get out of the blues and into the bliss.

THE BREATHING JOY MEDITATION

All of us get down in the dumps occasionally, and when we do, we normally want to get back to a joyful state as quickly as possible. This meditation is from the Buddhist *Sutra on Full Awareness of Breathing,* translated by Thich Nhat Hahn. A *sutra* is a written collection of the teachings of Buddha. We don't have to adhere to Buddhism or to any particular spiritual path to want more joy in our lives. This meditation works for everyone.

- Sit or lie down in your favorite meditation posture.

- Gently close your eyes and focus your inward gaze toward your heart.

- Make the intention that you are practicing this meditation to bring joy into your life.

- Focus on your breath for a minute or two to relax your body and quiet your mind.

- Becoming fully aware of your inhalation and exhalation, on the inhalation silently repeat:

I am breathing in and feeling joyful.

On the exhalation, silently repeat:

I am breathing out and feeling joyful.

- Continue this practice as long as you like.

- Rest for a few minutes when you are finished.

In addition to doing this as a formal meditation, you can repeat these phrases as you are going to sleep, as you do your manual chores, while walking, waiting in line, etc.

God will dance in our life when the day dawns in laughter and love.... True laughter — that is true prayer.

— SRI SRI RAVI SHANKAR

FOCUSING ON THE GOOD MEDITATION

When you are down and having a tough time thinking of anything good about yourself or your life, try this meditation to reconnect yourself to the remarkable human being that you truly are. Our lives are not about our achievements: What really matters is that we express the goodness that is within us.

- Sit or lie down in your favorite meditation posture.

- Gently close your eyes and focus your inward gaze toward your heart.

- Make the intention that you are practicing this meditation to remind yourself of your innate goodness and to further develop those virtues.

- Focus on your breath for a couple of minutes to allow your body and mind to relax.

- Concentrate on all the goodness that resides within you. Know that your heart is the center of your wisdom, kindness, compassion, humor, integrity, generosity, courage, patience, understanding, serenity, joy, and love. Know that these higher qualities are your true nature. Cherish yourself for who you truly are.

THE WATER MEDITATION

Depression is very common in our culture. Sometimes we are too depressed to even try to climb out of it. Next time you feel worried, tense, or down in the dumps, try this almost effortless technique.

- Find a body of water: an ocean, stream, lake, river, or a duck pond in the park.

- Sit next to this body of water and simply observe it. You will gradually become engrossed in the water's movement, as though it is a magnet. Just watch.

- Some time will pass and you will find that whatever it was you felt so glum about doesn't bother you anymore.

If some issues in your life are regularly getting you down but you can't change them at this time, try the water meditation on a regular basis. You will find that it helps the feelings of depression subside.

CULTIVATING THE GOOD MEDITATION

If you are having a tough time connecting with your goodness, or if you feel as though you need to further cultivate your innate goodness, try one or all of the following mantras.

- Sit or lie down in your favorite meditation posture.

- Gently close your eyes and focus your inward gaze toward your heart.

- Make the intention that you are practicing this meditation to remind yourself of your innate goodness and to further develop this quality.

- Focus on your breath for a couple of minutes to allow your body and mind to relax.

- Silently repeat the mantra that is most appropriate to your need. Below are some choices.

- Continue the meditation as long as you like.

Here are the mantras:

OM courage or I am courage.

OM patience or I am patience.

OM joy or I am joy.

OM love or I am love.

OM wisdom or I am wisdom.

OM peace or I am peace.

OM generosity or I am generosity.

OM compassion or I am compassion.

Acceptance Meditations

Full acceptance of our circumstances and of ourselves is a noble objective, but many of us experience a constant struggle between accepting who we are and wanting to improve ourselves. Sometimes we need to opt for the improved situation. For example, if we are in an abusive relationship or job, we must seek alternatives. At other times we need to embrace the dilemma we find ourselves in because that embrace, while painful, begins the process of growth, expansion, and reaching our full potential. Only our inner wisdom can guide us regarding what we need to accept and what we need to improve.

SELF-ACCEPTANCE MEDITATION

We have all heard that we must love our neighbors as we love ourselves. I've always thought this saying was a little odd, because most of us find it much easier to love and accept others than to love and accept ourselves.

If you are having difficulty accepting, valuing, and honoring yourself, try the following meditation. The intention of this meditation is to feel all the love you have for someone else and allow that love to do a U-turn and come back to you. You could not feel love for another if that love did not already exist within you. In this meditation, you surround yourself with your own love. If you have a persistent problem with self-acceptance, practice this meditation once or twice a week for several months.

- Sit or lie down in your favorite meditation position.

- Gently close your eyes and focus your inward gaze toward your heart.

- Make the intention that you are practicing this meditation to fully love and accept yourself.

- Focus on your breath for a minute or two to relax your body and quiet your mind.

- In your mind's eye, visualize the person you love the most. Vividly imagine him or her. Feel all of the love you have for this person. Experience the joy you feel when you are with this person. Don't hold back; totally immerse yourself in your love for this person. Project all of your love on this adored one. Honor, adore, cherish, appreciate, and delight in this person completely.

- Then allow the love you have for the other person to come back to you. Surround yourself with that love for yourself. Immerse yourself in your own capacity to love. Feel all of the adoration, reverence, and admiration you have for the other special person reflected to yourself. Not only do you deserve this type of love, but you could not possibly feel this kind of love for another unless that love already exists within you. Love is your true nature.

ACCEPTING LIFE MEDITATION

When you find yourself in a difficult but unchangeable situation, try this meditation instead of wishing it were different.

- Sit or lie down in your favorite meditation posture.

- Gently close your eyes and focus your inward gaze toward your heart.

- Make the intention that you are practicing this meditation to learn to accept life on its own terms.

- Focus on your breath for a minute or two to relax your body and quiet your mind.

- On your inhalation, silently repeat:

May I accept things as they are.

- On your exhalation, silently repeat:

May I enjoy serenity and peace.

- Continue the meditation as long as you like.

- In addition to doing this as a formal meditation, you can repeat these phrases as you are going to sleep, as you do your manual chores, while walking, waiting in line, etc.

Relationship Meditations

Our relationships give us our greatest joys and our deepest sorrows. The meditations in this section give you ways to deepen your love and ways to help you through the tough times.

The following meditations are specifically designed to strengthen our relationships with those closest to us. These meditations enhance our understanding, appreciation, respect, love, and compassion for each other. Try these with your partner, sibling, parent, or friend and see how quickly the relationship deepens.

I learned the two gazing meditations on a retreat given by the Art of Living Foundation. Each of us had an opportunity to gaze into every other participant's eyes. By the end of the practice, everyone felt tremendous love, kindness, and compassion for everyone else. However, when we first started, the gazing was a little awkward. You may also find this to be true. We are unaccustomed to looking deeply into another person's eyes, so when you practice this, give yourselves a few minutes to get through the uncomfortable stage. Laugh a little. Make some jokes if you like. But don't quit before giving yourself the opportunity to experience the benefits of these magnificent meditation techniques.

GAZING MEDITATION I

- Sit across from each other, either in chairs on or the floor, about 6 to 8 inches (15 to 20 cm) apart.

- Silently gaze into each other's eyes. Just look and see what you see. If the eyes are the windows of the soul, see what soulfulness is revealed in your partner's eyes.

- Just gaze. Without judgment, look deeply into your partner's eyes and allow yourself to see who he or she is. See the positives and the negatives and unconditionally accept your partner as he or she is.

- When you feel complete, bow to your partner, bowing to the Divine within him or her. Then, if you like, you can share your experiences with each other.

GAZING MEDITATION II

Try this meditation on a different day. It is really quite simple. Look into your partner's eyes and see all of his or her good qualities and let him or her know that you recognize his or her goodness.

- Sit across from each other, either in chairs on or the floor, about 6 to 8 inches (15 to 20 cm) apart.

- Gaze into each other's eyes. Just look and see what you see.

- Take turns telling your partner all of his or her good qualities.

- Allow the partner who is speaking to finish before the other begins.

- Take note whether any of those good qualities you see in your partner also exist within you.

BREATHING THE SAME BREATH MEDITATION

This technique is modified from Steve and Ondrea Levine's book *Embracing the Beloved*. It is a very loving, powerful, and bonding technique. I am grateful to them for sharing it.

- This exercise is to be done in silence.

- Partner A lies down while Partner B sits beside her.

- Partner B watches Partner A's breathing pattern for a few moments. Then B starts to synchronize his breath with Partner A's. It is as though both are breathing the same breath.

- Continue this for 5 to 15 minutes. When you feel complete, switch places.

- Partner B lies down and A sits next to B. A watches B's breath for a few moments and then starts to synchronize her breath with B's. Continue for 5 to 15 minutes, or until you feel complete.

- When you are finished, sit or lie together quietly for a few moments.

FOCUSING ON YOUR PARTNER'S STRENGTHS MEDITATION

The following meditation can be done when you are angry with or feeling distant from your partner, parent, sibling, or friend.

- Sit or lie down in your favorite meditation posture.

- Gently close your eyes and focus your inward gaze toward your heart.

- Make the intention that you are practicing this meditation to remind yourself of your partner's strengths and good qualities.

- Focus on your breath for a couple of minutes to relax your body and quiet your mind.

- Start to visualize your partner's face. Silently tell your partner all of his or her good qualities.

- Allow the list to take the form that is appropriate for your partnership. Acknowledge all of your partner's wonderful qualities. Let your intuition take you where it may.

- Here are examples of some things you can silently tell your partner:

You are kind.

You are loving.

You are a good father/mother.

You are understanding.

You have great integrity.

You are patient.

You are funny.

You are upbeat and happy.

You are generous.

You are a good cook.

You are a great handyman.

You always bring me coffee in the morning.

HEALING THE BREAKUP

Most of us have suffered deeply when we have ended a relationship. While we usually know that the breakup is for the best, the grieving period can still be very difficult. To soothe ourselves during these times, practice this version of The Loving-Kindness Meditation. You can also practice this meditation for your former partner, because he or she may also have a broken heart.

- Sit or lie down in your favorite meditation posture.

- Gently close your eyes and focus your inward gaze toward your heart.

- Make the intention that you are practicing this meditation to heal your heartbreak and/or your former partner's heartbreak.

- Focus on your breath for a minute or two to relax your body and quiet your mind.

- On the inhalation, silently repeat:

May I be free from suffering.

- On the exhalation, silently repeat:

May I be at peace.

- If meditating for your former partner, visualize his or her face. On the inhalation, silently repeat:

May you be free from suffering.

- On the exhalation, silently repeat:

May you be at peace.

- Continue the meditation as long as you like.

Meditations for Uncomfortable Situations

We all find ourselves in uncomfortable situations: business meetings, a family gathering, a meeting with our "ex," a day in court. Whatever the situation is, try one (or all) of these meditations to enhance your grace and poise. We usually know in advance that the situation is not going to be easy. So promise yourself that you will prepare by doing one of your favorite meditations and that you will also use one of the following meditations while you are in the fire, so you won't get singed.

BELLY-BREATHING MEDITATION

When we are in awkward situations, we unconsciously tighten our stomachs and our breathing becomes very shallow. So many of us hold onto so much stress that the use of anti-ulcer and anti-anxiety medications is prevalent. The breath is of paramount importance to our well-being. If we stop breathing or if our breathing is shallow, our body does not get the oxygen it needs, which causes more stress.

This meditation helps you become more aware of both your tummy and your breath. Concentrating on your breath and softening your tummy will put you more at ease, more in your own power. The relaxation you gain provides the clarity, insight, and perception you need in those difficult situations. Practice this meditation no matter where you are or what the situation is.

- When you start to feel anxious or upset, breathe deeply into your belly.

- Soften your belly with your breath. Take big belly breaths.

- Continue this deep breathing until you feel comfortable in the situation. Then return to normal breathing.

THE LOVE AND LIGHT MEDITATION

When you are in an uncomfortable situation, try this meditation. You will soon notice a change in your own comfort level and in the way others respond to you.

- Looking at the person or people in the room, imagine that your heart is emitting a ray of light, a rose-colored light of love or a golden light of healing.

- Imagine that this light is completely surrounding the people you are with.

- Imagine that the love and light from your own heart is also surrounding you.

- Know that your love is softening and healing the situation.

Forgiveness Meditations

Sometimes the most difficult aspects of forgiveness are finding a deep desire to forgive and believing that we truly can forgive. We convince ourselves that some things are simply unforgivable. But, of course, that is what forgiveness is all about — forgiving the unforgivable.

As time passes and we become aware that our lack of forgiveness is harming us as well as our relationships, the desire to fully forgive starts to develop. Though we want to forgive, we are not sure how. What we don't know until we actually do forgive is that forgiveness unburdens us, making us feel more free and joyful. This section offers forgiveness meditations and a meditation to increase our desire and our capacity to forgive.

NURTURING THE DESIRE TO FORGIVE

Nurturing your desire to forgive yourself or another person is often the first step in the forgiveness process. To nurture that desire to forgive and to increase your confidence that you truly can forgive yourself and others, try this meditation.

- Sit or lie down in your favorite meditation posture.

- Gently close your eyes and focus your inward gaze toward your heart.

- Make the intention that you are practicing this meditation so you can forgive _____ (fill in the name, and it may be your own name).

- Focus on your breath for a minute or two to relax your body and quiet your mind.

- On both the inhalation and the exhalation, silently repeat:

I truly want to forgive
_____.

- Other meditations to try are:

I know that I can truly forgive _____.

I know that I can completely forgive _____.

or

I can forgive
_____.

I can completely forgive
_____.

- If you synchronize the statements with your breath, the meditation becomes deeper and more powerful.

FORGIVING OTHERS MEDITATION

Often when we hurt others, we know that we did not intend to harm anyone. In other words, we assume our own innocence. So if we are innocent when we hurt others, why can't we assume someone else's innocence when they hurt us? Is it possible to believe that someone who has hurt us is innocent? Can we presume that this person has hurt us out of his or her own confusion, fear, anger or because he or she was hurt by someone else? Can we remember that we are all imperfect? We all make mistakes, sometimes truly atrocious mistakes. Allow the forgiveness to come into your own heart. Then forgive yourself for not being as forgiving as you would like to be.

Start first with your friends and family members, people who really love you, but who through carelessness or thoughtlessness have hurt you. Spouses and significant others are a good place to start because these are people we can most easily forgive. Later, we can work on the people who have hurt us more deeply.

- Sit or lie down in your favorite meditation posture.

- Gently close your eyes and focus your inward gaze toward your heart.

- Silently repeat:

My intention is to forgive _____ (fill in the name).

- Focus on your breath a minute or two to relax your body and quiet your mind.

- Visualize the person you want to forgive.

- On the inhalation silently repeat:

I forgive you.

- On the exhalation, silently repeat:

I open my heart to you.

- Continue the meditation as long as you like.

Your forgiveness should be such that the person who is being forgiven does not even know that you are forgiving them. They don't even feel guilty of a mistake. That is the right type of forgiveness.

— SRI SRI RAVI SHANKAR

FORGIVING YOURSELF MEDITATION

Sometimes we are just plain hard on ourselves. We may be quick to forgive others, but we can't forgive ourselves. Many of us feel excessively guilty about our mistakes.

Now is the time to stop condemning yourself for doing things that were not in your own best interest. Can you assume that at the time of your transgression, you were doing the best you could? Learn to love yourself as much as you love others. Don't be too hard on yourself for any mistake — mistakes are the way we learn. Remember that no one is perfect. Love yourself with all of your imperfections.

- Sit or lie down in your favorite meditation posture.

- Gently close your eyes and focus your inward gaze toward your heart.

- Silently repeat:

My intention is to forgive myself.

- Focus on your breath for a minute or two to relax your body and quiet your mind.

- Visualize yourself as someone who needs and deserves forgiveness.

- On the inhalation, silently repeat:

I forgive myself.

- On the exhalation, silently repeat:

I release all guilt.

- Another version you can practice is:

I forgive myself.
I accept myself as I am.

Developing Compassion

Compassion has three components. The first is a genuine concern for another's problem and the second is a sincere effort to help that person overcome the problem. This suggests compassion in action, which is what we do when we help others who are in need. The third component of compassion is an empathetic awareness of someone else's situation without explanation. For many of us, this is a more difficult aspect of compassion to internalize. This form of compassion reveals itself in us when someone is rude, abrupt, inconsiderate, sarcastic, or angry with us and we do not take offense because we know that deep inside he or she did not intend to hurt us. His action stems from being in an agitated emotional state. The person hurt us because he has been hurt himself.

Compassion goes beyond forgiveness. There is no need to forgive anyone when we are truly compassionate, because no one can hurt us. We sincerely see hurtful behavior toward us as an appeal for love, a cry of pain, and a fear of vulnerability.

COMPASSION MEDITATION

Compassion is natural in all of us. On some level we truly understand that every human being is part of us, part of our universal family. We may forget this as we go about our busy lives. In fact, we are often so busy and stressed that we become the one who needs compassion. The following meditation, which is a modified version of one taught by the Dalai Lama, reconnects us with our natural compassion for ourselves and for others.

- Sit or lie down in your favorite meditation posture.

- Gently close your eyes and focus your inward gaze toward your heart.

- Make the intention that you are practicing this meditation to develop compassion for yourself and others.

- Focus on your breath for a minute or two to relax your body and quiet your mind.

- Begin to feel love and compassion for yourself.

- As you inhale, feel a genuine compassion for yourself, a concern for your own problems. If it helps you can repeat the following:

I inhale compassion for myself.

- Visualize someone you know who is hurting physically or emotionally. On your exhalation, send that person compassion and concern for his problems. If it helps you can repeat the following:

I exhale compassion for _____.

- Continue the meditation for about 5 minutes. As you progress, you can increase the meditation time or you can meditate for several different people.

THE CIRCLE OF COMPASSION MEDITATION

This meditation is very easy and can be practiced all day long: with your family, at the supermarket, at the car wash, in a business meeting, on the subway, at a dinner party, etc. It is a great reminder to encompass everyone we see with compassion.

- At the beginning of your day, make the intention that you will embrace everyone you see with compassion.

- Wherever you are, whatever you are doing, imagine a circle of compassion around you. Visualize the circumference of this circle of compassion as 500 feet (155 m) around you.

- If you like, you can give it a color: pink, blue, gold, white.

- All day long, be aware of this compassion within you, around you, and encompassing everyone within 500 feet of you.

- Consciously surround everyone you see with your circle of compassion.

TONGLEN MEDITATION

Tonglen is the most well-known and most often practiced Buddhist meditation for cultivating compassion. Buddhists express compassion as a genuine concern for another's suffering and a willingness to help relieve that suffering. Compassion is the highest goal of a devout Buddhist and is more important than personal enlightenment. Buddhists believe that none of us are fully enlightened until we are all free from suffering. Buddhist teachings are full of Bodhisattvas, people who are about to become enlightened but who instead choose to stay on earth to help liberate others from suffering.

Tonglen is the "receiving–giving" or "taking–sending" meditation in which we relieve and heal the suffering of others by receiving their pain and giving them our joy, wisdom, love, and kindness. Tonglen helps those for whom we meditate and it helps us transform our own personal suffering into a tender, heart-felt concern for others and for ourselves. In practicing Tonglen, we transcend our tendency to think primarily about our own problems and we increase our capacity to care about the problems of others.

Everyone understands the selfless love parents have for their children. Most parents would willingly sacrifice their own well-being in order to take on their child's suffering. By practicing Tonglen *we can* take on the suffering of our loved ones and relieve their pain.

Another way to practice Tonglen is to use the suffering we are currently experiencing — a broken heart, a serious injury or illness, money fears, etc. If we think of others who have problems that are similar to ours and meditate with them in mind, we ease the tension we create around our own problem. We also open our hearts to others and help them feel more calm and peaceful.

The instructions here are intended for practicing Tonglen for your loved ones. Modify the meditation appropriately for other situations.

- Prepare for meditation as you normally do.

- Begin to think of your loved one and the suffering he is experiencing. Allow yourself to fully and completely feel his pain, as though it were your own.

- As you inhale, imagine that you are inhaling his pain and suffering.

- On your exhalation, visualize that you are healing him. Give him your loving-kindness, happiness, wisdom, and mercy. Sincerely feel the desire to end his pain. Send all of your resources — physical, emotional, spiritual, and material — to heal his pain.

- Expect that your ability to heal him is a fact. Know deep in your soul that as you inhale you take on his suffering and as you exhale you are sending him inner peace and physical healing.

- If it helps, you can imagine your exhalation of healing as a white light.

- Continue this practice for approximately 5 minutes. Increase the time period when you are ready.

- First practice Tonglen for your loved ones; then expand your practice to include a wider and wider circle of people. Ultimately you will develop a sincere compassion for all people, even those who have hurt you deeply.

Notes for practice: *If you have difficulty sending all of your resources to heal the other person, you might try exhaling one or two strengths. For example, if someone you know is in a difficult situation and is experiencing a lot of fear, inhale his fear and send him courage and determination. If someone you know is very sad, receive her sadness on your inhalation and give her your joy.*

When you are practicing Tonglen for those you don't know, trust that what you send will be transformed into exactly what they need: food for the hungry, medical care for the sick and the injured, money for the poor, peace for the emotionally distraught, etc. To learn more about Tonglen, refer to Pema Chodron's books and tapes.

The difference among faiths is only one in names;

everywhere the yearning is for the same God.

— KABIR

No meditation book would be complete without an exploration of meditation's spiritual roots. The mystical traditions of all religions advocate meditation as a spiritual practice. There is no historical evidence to tell us when or how meditation practices began, but we know that some meditation traditions originated at least 5000 years ago and were kept alive through oral instruction from teacher to student.

5

Going Deeper: The Spiritual Aspect of Meditation

As we progress in meditation, we experience something beyond our ordinary existence. This "something beyond" is what many people call God. Accordingly, I use the term *God* throughout this book. For clarification, I would like to explain what I mean by God.

First and foremost, I have no idea what God is. God is a mystery and while we can accept mysteries, we can never truly understand them — mysteries transcend reason. The Christian mystic, St. Thomas Aquinas, reminds us that when we speak of God we can only speak in analogies. In light of this, I use the term *God* as a synonym for:

- the totality of existence
- the creative force
- the underlying reality
- the ultimate reality
- universal energy
- universal reality
- the ultimate truth

God is *Life* itself. God is the substratum of the universe, the foundation of all existence. God is the ground of our being, the basis of all life. God is consciousness —

Cosmic Consciousness and our own individual core consciousness.

Some religions call God "the Supreme" or "the Absolute." Most spiritual traditions claim that God is omnipresent — that is, God is everywhere and in everything. Following that line of reasoning, God is indeed everything. Our entire universe is God — every star, planet, cloud, river, field, and plant. Every animate being and every inanimate object is part of God. There is nothing that is not God. God is in us and we are in God.

Other religions maintain a belief that God and man are separate. This dualistic nature fosters a devotional relationship in man toward God and allows for a deity who can intervene on man's behalf.

Some religions do not profess concepts of God. Buddhists, for example, do not use the term *God* and don't believe in a creative force. They believe in an Underlying Reality and that the world in which we live has always existed and continues to expand. Lao Tzu, the Chinese philosopher who wrote the *Tao Te Ching*, referred to the mystery of life as the *Tao* and said, "The Tao that can be known is not the true Tao." Although

different traditions use different terminology, I think that all the appellations are simply names for the same thing — the indefinable mystery of life, or God.

New scientific research suggests that our brains are programmed to look for and to understand God. Central to all spiritual practices is the inner search for God, the Tao, or Underlying Reality within ourselves. That is where meditation comes in. Through meditation it is possible to experience God. For example, we may have a vision of our favorite deity or we may feel eternal love or we may experience a completely still mind. It is just as likely, however, that as we continue our meditation practice all of our concepts of God will be shattered.

My best advice for understanding God, the incomprehensible mystery, comes from the Sufi mystic Abd al-Qadir al Jilani, who said, "Each time that something comes to your mind regarding Allah (God) — know that He is different from that!" The most important thing about meditation and spiritual experience is to have no expectations. Grace comes when we least expect it, not when we are looking for it.

HINDUISM

Brahman is that which is immutable and independent of any cause but itself. The creative energy of Brahman is that which causes all existences to come into being.

— BHAGAVAD GITA

The original name for Hinduism was *sanatana dharma,* meaning "righteousness that has no beginning or end." The eternal truths of Hinduism were divinely inspired, revealed to learned meditation masters called *rishis.* Some accounts date the Vedas, the earliest Hindu writings, to the end of the last Ice Age, approximately 11,600 years ago. Other accounts date their origin at 6000 to 7000 B.C., and still others date it at roughly 3000 B.C. Whatever the date, they remain some of the earliest written records of man's quest for spirituality.

Hinduism is considered the mother of all religions, partly because it is the oldest living religion and also because Hinduism has given birth to many other religions: Buddhism, Jainism, and Sikhism. Many Hindus claim the saviors and prophets of other religions as their own, believing that Buddha, Christ, and Muhammad were incarnations of the Hindu deity Vishnu. Hindus see all spiritual traditions as true and valid.

Hindus believe in a Universal Reality, which is formless and indefinable. God as the Universal Reality is called *Brahman.* Because Brahman is omnipresent, it is within all sentient beings and all inanimate objects. Residing in the individual, this Universal Reality is called the *atman.* The translation of *atman* is "the real self." Where we are on our path to understanding Universal Reality is called *karma.* Karma is the law of consequence with regard to actions. Karma is also considered to be the sum of all our thoughts and actions in this life and previous lives. Because of karma, man has forgotten his true nature — his inner divinity.

While Hindus believe in one Universal Reality, the Hindu pantheon boasts thousands of gods, each representing an aspect of Brahman. Some deities represent ideal characteristics that, through meditation, can be realized and perfected in each and every individual.

Hindu Meditation

In Hinduism, meditation is practiced to quiet and clear the mind, thus allowing us see our true nature, which is atman (the real or true self). Through meditation, we see that we are not separate from God, but rather one with God or Brahman.

In Hinduism, there are several practices that can be done to prepare oneself for meditation. Included in these are yoga exercises and pranayama, the discipline of controlled breathing. Among its many benefits, a regular practice of yoga and pranayama helps quiet and focus the mind, allowing the peace of meditation to occur naturally.

Mantra meditation is the most common Hindu meditation practice. A mantra is a sacred word, syllable, or phrase that changes the internal energy of the meditator and the energy of the environment.

Many of the mantras that are used today come from the Vedas and were passed down orally for thousands of years prior to their inscription.

Some mantras are one-syllable sounds, called "seed mantras." Seed mantras have no exact meaning; rather, they invoke an experience of Brahman. The most recognizable example of a seed mantra is *OM*. Other mantras contain many words and are used to invoke the qualities or grace of a particular deity to effect changes in one's life.

Mantras can be repeated silently or aloud. Chanting the mantras aloud tunes us in or harmonizes us to the energy of the divine quality we are seeking to develop, the situation we are seeking to change, or the spiritual knowledge we wish to experience.

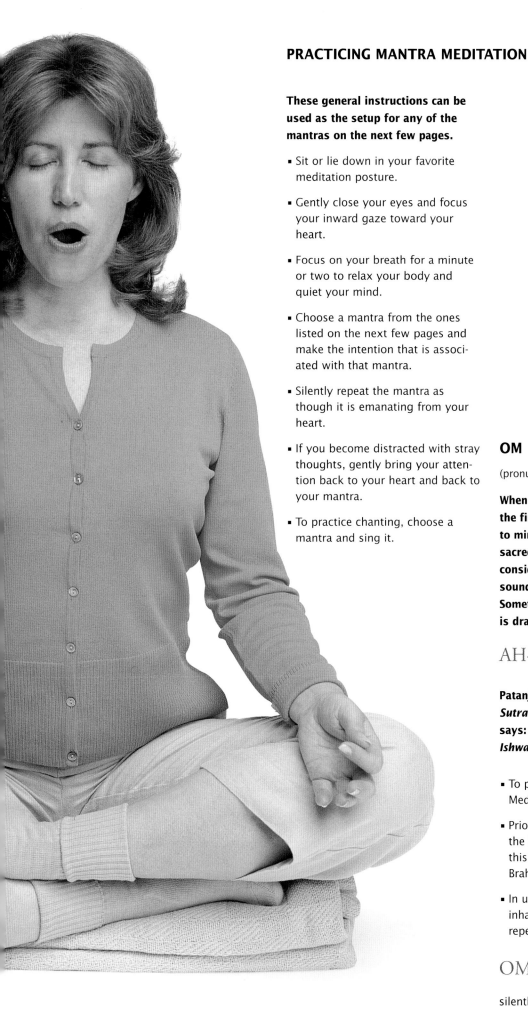

PRACTICING MANTRA MEDITATION

These general instructions can be used as the setup for any of the mantras on the next few pages.

- Sit or lie down in your favorite meditation posture.

- Gently close your eyes and focus your inward gaze toward your heart.

- Focus on your breath for a minute or two to relax your body and quiet your mind.

- Choose a mantra from the ones listed on the next few pages and make the intention that is associated with that mantra.

- Silently repeat the mantra as though it is emanating from your heart.

- If you become distracted with stray thoughts, gently bring your attention back to your heart and back to your mantra.

- To practice chanting, choose a mantra and sing it.

OM

(pronunciation: OH-M or AH-OH-MM)

When most of us think of a mantra, the first thing that normally comes to mind is *OM*. OM is the most sacred symbol in Hinduism. *OM* is considered the sound of God or the sound of Universal Consciousness. Sometimes *OM* is spelled AUM and is drawn out into three syllables:

AH-OO-MM

Patanjali, who wrote *The Yoga Sutras,* a classical text on yoga, says: "Meditate on OM to contact *Ishwara* (God). It is his symbol."

- To prepare, see Practicing Mantra Meditation above.

- Prior to using this mantra, make the intention that you are repeating this mantra to become one with Brahman.

- In using this mantra, take a normal inhalation, and on your exhalation repeat

OM

silently or aloud.

SO HUM

(pronunciation: SO-HUM)

The translation of this phrase is: "I am that which is all there is." In other words, the meditator is one with Brahman.

- To prepare, see Practicing Mantra Meditation above.

- Prior to using this mantra, make the intention that you are using this mantra to unite you with everything and everyone around you.

- When practicing this mantra, on the inhalation silently repeat

SO

and on the exhalation silently repeat

HUM

OM NAMAH SHIVAYA

(pronunciation: OM NAH-MAH SHE-VAH-YAH)

Necessary props:
photo of yourself, something to put photo on

There are two common translations for this mantra. One is: "I bow to the Divine within." This reminds us that God is within everything and everyone, including ourselves. It helps us identify with — and nurture — our own divine nature. *Om Namah Shivaya* is also translated as "I bow to the Lord Shiva." Shiva is the deity who represents Universal Reality or Supreme Consciousness. Thus, this mantra is used both to honor and praise God and as an invocation to God to more fully manifest within us.

This mantra is often used as a purifying mantra. In other words, as we practice this mantra our individual consciousness is cleansed of negativity, so our divine essence, or atman, can more fully manifest.

- To prepare, see Practicing Mantra Meditation on page 91.

- Prior to chanting this mantra or using it in meditation, make the intention that you are practicing this mantra to purify your consciousness and allow Universal Reality to fully manifest.

- In silent repetition of this mantra, on the inhalation repeat

OM Namah

and on the exhalation, repeat

Shivaya

HARE KRISHNA

(pronunciation: AH-RAY KREESH-NAH)

Krishna is the Hindu god of love. *Hare,* which means "stealer of hearts," is an innocent, sincere, and loving way a devotee addresses the Lord. When we experience the Divine in any form, we fall deeply and passionately in love with God. We experience unrivaled joy, and the Lord of Love completely steals our hearts.

- To prepare, see Practicing Mantra Meditation on page 91.

- Prior to chanting this mantra or using it in silent meditation, make

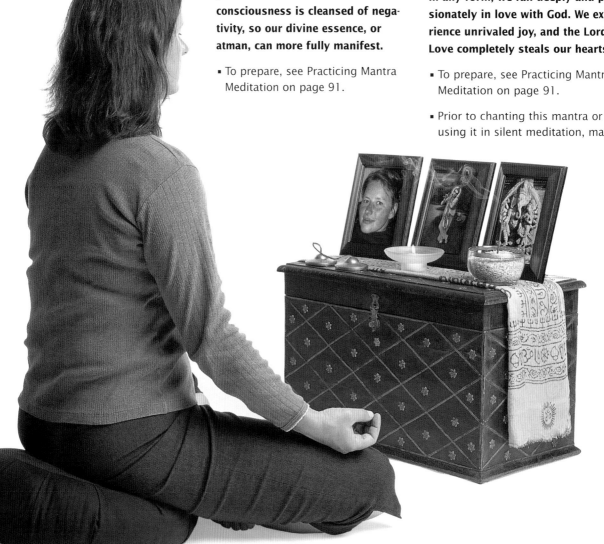

the intention that you are petitioning Lord Krishna to grace you with his love and presence. In using this mantra, we deepen our connection to the Divine and more fully connect to the love and joy that reside within us.

- In chanting this mantra, you might want to chant in this way:

Krishna, Krishna — Hare Krishna

In silent meditation, on the inhalation repeat

Hare

and on the exhalation, repeat

Krishna

SRI MAHA LAKSHMI NAMOH NAMAH

(pronunciation: SHREE MAH-HA LAKSH-MEE NAH-MO NA-MAH-HA)

An approximate English translation of this mantra is: "I bow to the great goddess Lakshmi, goddess of abundance." Lakshmi, the goddess of spiritual and material prosperity, is a favorite goddess of the Hindus. She usually is depicted standing or seated on a lotus blossom with gold coins coming out of her hands. The coins, of course, symbolize material wealth. The lotus flower, floating on the water, symbolizes spiritual liberation. Two white elephants are often pictured with Lakshmi. They symbolize the need to share our wealth with others so everyone can be happy.

- To prepare, see Practicing Mantra Meditation above.
- Prior to repeating this mantra, make the intention that you are seeking material abundance, spiritual abundance, or both.

- In practicing this mantra, on the inhalation silently repeat

Sri Maha Lakshmi

and on the exhalation, silently repeat

Namoh Namaha

OM SRI GANESHA NAMAH

(pronunciation: OM SHREE GAH-NESH-A NA-MAH-HA)

Ganesha is the ever-popular elephant-headed god. His name means "he who removes all obstacles." Hindus invoke his grace at the start of any ceremony and at the start of a new venture: a wedding, a new home, a new business, a new child, and at the start of the New Year. Ganesha will give you what you sincerely ask for, unless what you are asking for is not for your highest good. His trunk hangs between two tusks, signifying the balance between the material world and spirituality. If you ask him, he will grace you with the touch of his trunk and will smash all obstacles in your path. Ganesha reminds us that the Divine resides in every living being.

- To prepare, see Practicing Mantra Meditation above.
- Prior to practicing this mantra, make the intention that you are seeking the removal of obstacles in attaining your goal: a new job, a new home, a new relationship, or whatever it may be.

- In practicing, on the inhalation silently repeat

OM Sri Ganesha

and on the exhalation silently repeat

Namah

SRI RAM, JAI RAM

(pronunciation: SHREE RAHM, JAY RAHM)

The approximate English translation for this mantra is: "Hail Rama, Victory to Rama." Rama is an incarnation of Vishnu, the Hindu god of preservation. Rama is known for being an expert with the bow and arrow, which he considers sacred. He performed his miracles with his divine arrows. When chanting to Rama, allow his Divine arrows to pierce your heart — and release all the love that resides within you.

- To prepare, see Practicing Mantra Meditation above.
- Prior to chanting this mantra or using it in silent meditation, make the intention that you are practicing this mantra to help open your heart to yourself and to others.
- In silent meditation, on the inhalation repeat

Sri Ram

and on the exhalation repeat

Jai Ram

- When chanting the name of Rama, allow his divine arrows to pierce your heart and release all of the love, kindness, and compassion that reside within you.

BUDDHISM

Buddhism is a philosophy and a religion that originated with an Indian prince — Siddhartha Gautama — who lived from 563 to 483 B.C. At the time of his birth, Siddhartha's parents were told that their son would either be a great king who would unify the world or a world redeemer. Siddhartha's father, the king, naturally wanted his son to become the next great king, so he sheltered him and did his utmost to make sure that he was completely happy. It was not until he was a young man that Siddhartha escaped the confines of the palace and saw the pain and suffering of the townspeople.

Upon seeing hunger, sickness, and death, Siddhartha was no longer content with his regal life. Siddhartha escaped from the palace, leaving his wife and child behind. He was determined to find a way to release mankind from its pain and suffering. Siddhartha studied with various Hindu masters and lived as an ascetic. His monastic practices were so severe that he was on the verge of death when his companions fed him and saved his life. Having experienced the opulent palace life and severe asceticism, Siddhartha developed a new philos-

ophy he called the *Middle Way*, which simply says: give the body what it needs, but do not indulge it.

One afternoon Siddhartha sat meditating beneath a fig tree (popularly known as the Bodhi tree), and vowed to remain there until he reached full spiritual illumination. After a night filled with temptations and death threats from Mara (an evil deity), Siddhartha was transformed into the Buddha — the *Awakened One*.

Buddha explained his experiences under the Bodhi tree with the Four Noble Truths and the Noble Eightfold Path.

The First Noble Truth is that life contains suffering and we need to be in touch with our suffering — we must not deny its existence or run away from it.

The Second Noble Truth is that we should look deeply into our suffering, which is caused by our attachments, desires, and cravings for impermanent and ultimately unsatisfactory things.

The Third Noble Truth is that escape from suffering is possible by eliminating our attachments, desires, and cravings.

The Fourth Noble Truth is that there is a path that assists us in stopping the things that are causing our suffering. This is the Noble Eightfold Path, which includes: Right View, Right Thinking, Right Mindfulness, Right Speech, Right Action, Right Effort, Right Concentration, and Right Livelihood.

Buddha challenged the teachings of Hinduism. He encouraged individuals to come into their own enlightenment, not through the guidance of a priest, a guru, or even the gods. Rather, each person must attain liberation by his own practice of meditation and by serving others. The Buddha provided individuals with a way to attain enlightenment in their own lifetime, rather than having to go through multiple lifetimes as suggested by traditional Hindus.

Buddhism teaches that there is an *Underlying Reality* that permeates all of existence. This reality is beyond our intellectual comprehension and can only be experienced by practicing meditation. A continual experience of this understanding is called *nirvana* or *Emptiness*.

Buddha insisted that he was not

God, that he was merely "awake" and did not want to be worshipped as God. Theoretically, there are no gods or deities in Buddhism. Yet iconography of Buddhist deities is prevalent. Many of the deities are considered *bodhisattvas,* beings who are very close to their own enlightenment who, out of compassion, stay on earth to help relieve suffering and to help others gain enlightenment.

Many of the deities are different aspects of the Buddha — there are Buddhas of Wisdom, Buddhas of Medicine, Healing Buddhas, and Teaching Buddhas. There are both male and female Buddhas. These icons are used to remind practitioners of the qualities they would like to cultivate in themselves — wisdom, compassion, healing, deep listening, benevolence, etc. Many Buddhist practitioners believe that the deities are a manifestation of Emptiness and discard them when they no longer need them for inspiration.

Buddhist Meditation

The ultimate goal of Buddhism is *nirvana,* which means "extinction." This state, also called *Emptiness,* is achieved through meditation, which is fundamental in all schools of Buddhism. In Buddhism, meditation is a means to develop self-awareness and self-knowledge. It helps us gain an understanding of consciousness itself — our own consciousness and ultimately an intuitive understanding of Underlying Reality. A continual experience of Emptiness or nothingness is nirvana or enlightenment. This is the state in which our own individual consciousness merges with Underlying Reality or *Buddha Nature.*

Buddhists practice meditation to develop *mindfulness* and to allow our innate compassion to unfold. Mindfulness allows us to be completely aware in each and every moment, without thinking of anything other than what we are currently doing. Mindfulness brings more energy and concentration into the present moment, without distracting thoughts of the past or future.

Through meditation we gain insight into the nature of the mind.

This takes place on many levels. On one level, we begin to understand both our positive and negative qualities and we learn to accept ourselves and others without blame or judgment. Through various meditation practices, we nurture and develop our positive qualities by connecting with our core consciousness, which is infinitely loving, kind, and compassionate. By connecting to this *core consciousness,* we become more compassionate toward ourselves and toward others. In becoming more compassionate, we then actively seek to relieve the suffering of all others.

Buddhist meditation takes several forms, including:

- following the breath

- guided meditations to nurture our positive qualities

- mantra meditation.

WATCHING THE BREATH

The practice of sitting and watching the breath is a primary meditation practice in all schools of Buddhism. Watching the breath helps us connect to the present moment and understand the nature of the mind. This practice is traditionally done in a seated posture and with the eyes cast downward but not closed. However, Kunzig Shamar Rinpoche, the present Sharmapa of the Karma Kaygu Buddhist tradition, told me that it is okay for beginners to close their eyes while meditating; and if you are lying down, it is essential.

- Sit or lie down in your favorite meditation posture.

- If seated, gently close your eyes or allow your gaze to be cast downward a few inches (5 or 7 cm) in front of you. If you are lying down, your eyes should be completely closed.

- Make the intention that you are practicing this meditation to develop mindfulness, to become more aware of the mind's true nature, and to connect with your core consciousness.

- Become completely aware of your body.

- Breathing normally, start to focus your attention on your breath. You can choose a particular place to focus. For example, you can focus

your attention at the tip of your nose or you can watch the rise and fall of your abdomen. You can watch the breath as it enters your nose, goes through your mouth and throat, through your chest and stomach, and then makes its way back up and out of the nose.

- If your mind starts to wander, simply bring your attention back to your breath.

- The late Tibetan Buddhist teacher Choygam Trungpa Rinpoche advised his students to have a "light" focus on the breath. In other words, don't become tense or stressed as you follow your breath. Keep a light attitude.

- Continue this practice for 3 to 5 minutes. Increase the meditation time as you feel ready, eventually practicing for 20 to 30 minutes.

Buddhism offers many wonderful prayers and meditations to help us transform suffering, both our own and that of others, into compassion and loving-kindness. Here are a few of these very special meditations.

THE RIGHT SPEECH MEDITATION

This prayer is from the Fourth Mindfulness Training, which reminds us to speak and to listen with love, compassion, and kindness.

- Sit or lie down in your favorite meditation posture.
- Gently close your eyes or allow your gaze to be cast downward toward a copy of the meditation.
- Make the intention that you are doing this practice to help you cultivate loving, compassionate communication.
- Focus on your breath for a minute or two to relax your body and quiet your mind.
- Recite the following prayer, silently or aloud, repeating it as many times as you like.

Aware of the suffering caused by unmindful speech and the inability to listen to others, I am committed to cultivating loving speech and deep listening in order to bring joy and happiness to others and relieve others of their suffering. Knowing that words can create happiness or suffering, I am determined to speak truthfully, with words that inspire self-confidence, joy, and hope. I will not spread news that I do not know to be certain and will not criticize or condemn things of which I am not sure. I will refrain from uttering words that can cause division or discord, or that can cause the family or the community to break. I am determined to make all efforts to reconcile and resolve all conflicts, however small.*

*This version is from *The Heart of the Buddha's Teachings,* Thich Nhat Hahn, Broadway Books, 1998.

THE SIX PARAMITAS MEDITATION

The Six Paramitas, or the Six Perfections, are virtues that all of us try to cultivate to improve our relationship with ourselves and with others. This practice helps us manifest these qualities more readily. In her book *Tap Dancing in Zen*, the delightful Zen Buddhist dharma teacher Geri Larkin calls them "The Six Fingers of Zen." We can count these prayers on our fingers as we recite them, and by doing so, we can count on transforming ourselves into kinder, more loving people. You can repeat one or all of these during your normal meditation time, or you can repeat them as you brush your teeth, cook, clean, do errands, etc. Different versions are taught by different Buddhist teachers. This one is Geri Larkin's.

- Sit in your favorite meditation posture.

- Gently close your eyes or allow your gaze to be cast downward toward a copy of the meditation.

- Make the intention that you are practicing this meditation to nurture your fundamental goodness.

- Focus on your breath for a minute or two to relax your body and quiet your mind.

- Silently repeat one or all of these phrases as many times as you like.

- Another method is to practice one for a few days, then move on to the second for a few days, then the third, and so on.

1. May I be generous and helpful.

2. May I be pure and virtuous.

3. May I be patient. May I be able to bear and forbear the wrongs of others.

4. May I be strenuous, energetic, and persevering.

5. May I practice meditation and attain concentration and oneness to serve all beings.

6. May I gain wisdom and be able to give the benefits of my wisdom to others.

Buddhist Mantra Meditation

Mantra meditation practice is very important in Tibetan Buddhism but is not always stressed in other schools of Buddhism.

OM MANI PADME HUM

(pronunciation: OM MAH-NEE PAHD-MAY HOOM)

The primary mantra Tibetan Buddhists use is *OM mani padme HUM.* The translation is "The jewel is in the lotus" or "Praise to the jewel in the lotus." The jewel is considered to be Underlying Reality, Consciousness, or Buddha Nature and the lotus is often interpreted as our own individual heart. In practicing this mantra, we are attempting to purify and transform our consciousness into the consciousness of a Buddha.

- Sit in your favorite meditation posture.

- Gently close your eyes or allow your gaze to be cast downward a few inches (5 or 7 cm) in front of you.

- Make the intention that you are practicing this meditation to uncover your Buddha nature.

- Focus your attention on your breath for a minute or two to relax your body and quiet your mind.

- Silently repeat the mantra for about 5 minutes:

OM mani padme HUM

- When you have finished, lie down and rest.

- As you progress in your meditation practice, you can increase the time spent in this meditation to 10 minutes and then up to 20 or 30 minutes.

MANTRA FOR THE PLANET: HUNG VAJRA PEH

(pronunciation: HOONG VAHJ-RAH PAY)

In Tibetan Buddhism, it is believed that there are negative energy "pockets" that surround the earth. These are the result of anger, violence, wars, and other offensive behavior. To help purify the planet, we can repeat the mantra to Vajrapani, the deity of protection. He is also known as the Great Initiator because he reveals life's mysteries to the sincere spiritual seeker. In repeating this mantra, we invoke his blessing to remove negative energy from our planet.

- Sit in your favorite meditation posture.

- Gently close your eyes or allow your gaze to be cast downward a few inches (5 or 7 cm) in front of you.

- Make the intention that you are practicing this mantra to help purify the negative energy in our world.

- Focus your attention on your breath for a minute or two to relax your body and quiet your mind.

- Silently repeat the mantra for about 5 minutes:

Hung Vajra Peh

- When you have finished, lie down and rest.

- As you progress in your meditation practice, you can increase the time spent in this meditation to 10 minutes and then up to 20 or 30 minutes.

MANTRA FOR PURIFICATION: OM VAJRASATTVA HUNG

(pronounced: OM VAHJ-RAH SAHT-VAH HOONG)

This mantra is used to purify our own consciousness. It invokes the blessing and protection of Vajrasattva, the deity known to Tibetan Buddhists as The Great Purifier. When someone practices this mantra, he usually visualizes Vajrasattva pouring white light into his head, releasing negative thoughts and habits. This version is modified, but you can change it if you like by visualizing Vajrasattva or your favorite deity pouring white light into your head.

- Sit in your favorite meditation posture.

- Gently close your eyes or allow your gaze to be cast downward a few inches in front of you.

- Make the intention that you are practicing this meditation to purify yourself by releasing negative thoughts and habits.

- Focus your attention on your breath for a minute or two to help relax the body and focus the mind.

- Visualize a ball of radiant white light above your head. Imagine that this white light is entering your head and dispelling all negative thought patterns.

- Silently repeat the mantra for about 5 minutes:

OM Vajrasattva Hung

- When you have finished, lie down and rest.

- As you progress in your meditation practice, you can increase the time spent in this meditation to 10 minutes and then up to 20 or 30 minutes.

TAOISM

*All things return to the Tao
As the river flows down to the sea.*

— LAO TZU

Taoism is based on the *Tao Te Ching* (pronounced "Dow De Jing"), which means *The Power and Its Way*. The *Tao Te Ching* was written by the Chinese philosopher Lao Tzu, who was born in about 600 B.C. Lao Tzu worked as a curator in the archives of the Chou dynasty. It is said that Lao Tzu was Confucius' teacher and that in his presence people were healed of their injuries and illnesses.

The time in which Lao Tzu lived was one of the most intellectually creative periods in Chinese history. Yet internal strife and war with neighboring provinces were widespread. Lao Tzu was saddened by his contemporaries' unwillingness to make peace with their neighbors and their reluctance to cultivate their own natural goodness. Consequently, Lao Tzu decided to leave his province. As he was passing through the town gates, the gatekeeper, aware of Lao Tzu's efforts to bring peace and harmony to the region, tried to persuade him to stay. Lao Tzu repeatedly refused, so the gatekeeper finally asked him to at least write down his philosophy for the civilization he was leaving behind. He agreed to do so and within a few days produced his succinct philosophy.

The *Tao Te Ching*, which remains the basic text of all Taoist thought, contains approximately 5000 words in 81 poetic verses. This brief, mysterious, and extremely profound text is the basis of a philosophy that has endured 25 centuries and is continually gaining popularity.

The simplest explanation of Taoism is this: there is a universal force in the world called the *Tao*. The Tao is a mystery and we can never fully understand it. However, if we align ourselves with the Tao, our lives will flow as easily as water flows downhill. Water gently melts away rock and carves new pathways. With its force, the sharp edges of stones soften and become round and polished. If we align ourselves with the Tao, our sharp edges will also disappear and the Tao will gently melt obstacles that are in our path.

It is important to remember that water flowing downhill takes many things with it: beautiful leaves as well as discarded soda cans. Flowing water also knows what it can't carry — rocks and trees, for example. We must remember to accept what life gives us, the beautiful and the not so beautiful. We must also be aware of what we can and cannot carry.

A life aligned with the Tao is called *wu wei*. While *wu wei* has been called "do-nothingness," the concept might better be described as the "effortless effort." If we are one with the Tao, everything we need will naturally come to us. Our work, our creativity, our relationships will flow effortlessly. Lao Tzu's advice is, "The way to do is simply to be." Allow the Tao to flow in and out of your life, and your life becomes a dance of balance and grace.

Taoism is a very moral, just, and simple philosophy. The *Tao Te Ching* advocates nonviolence, noncompetition, patience, kindness, humility, health, and respect for nature and the environment. While these qualities can be practiced, if we become one with the Tao, these qualities naturally govern our behavior.

Taoism sees everyone as part of the Tao, and as such, we are all one with each other. Much of the *Tao Te Ching* advocates pacifism and gives practical advice for cultivating peace. These words are as meaningful today as they were 2500 years ago.

Taoist Meditation

Be good to those who are good
And to those who are not.
For goodness increases goodness.
Have faith in those who are faithful
And in those who are not.
For faith brings greater faith
And goodness and faith build peace.

— LAO TZU

The intention of Taoist meditation is to empty the mind, thus allowing insights into the mystery of life and unity with the Tao. Taoist sitting meditation is very similar to the Buddhist Watching the Breath Meditation.

Other forms of meditation include breathing techniques and movement exercises called qi gong. Practitioners stimulate and strengthen the body's vital energy — called *qi* or *chi* — and keep it moving harmoniously throughout the body. Chi can stagnate if not kept flowing, causing physical, emotional, and spiritual disease.

Qi gong is primarily a moving meditation. In intent it is similar to the discipline of yoga exercises. Both techniques balance the nervous system, lower blood pressure, relieve stress, enhance digestion, improve blood circulation, improve the functions of the internal organs, and quiet the mind. While qi gong is beyond the scope of this book, below is a very simple qi gong meditation.

BELOW-THE-NAVEL BREATHING

This meditation balances the chi and allows it to flow throughout your body.

- Lie down on your back, either on the floor or on your bed. Use a pillow for your head or neck and, if needed, one under your thighs to eliminate any pressure on your lower back.

- Gently close your eyes and focus your attention just below your navel.

- Make the intention that you are practicing this meditation to strengthen your chi, your vital energy.

- Place the fingers of one hand about 2 inches (5 cm) below your navel. The placement may vary by a half-inch (1 cm) or so depending on the length of your torso.

- Breathing normally, concentrate your breath in that area. Breathe into the area below your navel and breathe out from that area.

- You will soon start to feel a release of energy from your navel area. You may feel the energy moving into your torso or into your legs.

- Continue the breathing as long as you like, perhaps starting with 5 minutes and, as you feel ready, increase the time to as much as 20 minutes.

- When you are finished, continue lying down for a few minutes to rest.

To the mind that is still, the whole universe surrenders.

— LAO TZU

EMPTYING THE MIND

As we all know, emptying the mind is not an easy task. The intent of this meditation is to make that process easier.

- Sit or lie down in your favorite meditation posture.

- Gently close your eyes.

- Make the intention that you are practicing this meditation to help empty your mind and allow the Tao to make its home within you.

- Focus on your breath for a minute or two to relax your body and quiet your mind.

- Scan your body to determine where you can best feel your breath. The most commonly felt places are at the end of your nostrils as you inhale and exhale or your abdomen as it rises and falls.

- Choose either of these spots and focus your attention there. Just watch the breath — in and out of the nostrils or up and down in the belly.

- While you are meditating, you will have thoughts and lose track of your breath. That is normal. Once you realize you are distracted, simply bring your focus back to your breath, inhaling and exhaling, rising and falling.

- If you have been sitting, lie down for a few minutes and rest.

- If you are new to meditation, try this for about 5 minutes. If you like the practice, over time you can extend the length of time to 10 minutes and then to 15 or 20 minutes.

Bide in silence and the radiance of the spirit will come in and make its home.

— LAO TZU

THE YIN-YANG MEDITATION

It is said that if you meditate on the yin-yang symbol, the world's mysteries will be revealed to you. The yin-yang symbol represents life's opposites: good and evil, darkness and light, positive and negative, sickness and health, masculine and feminine. There is a circle of light in the center of the dark section and a circle of darkness inside the light half. Within this symbol, opposites lose their meaning. Do we truly know what is good and what is evil? Can we truly call something evil if good results from it? When we are sick, can we remember our health? When we are healthy, can we remember that sickness is part of life? When we are experiencing difficulties, can we remember that good times will return? And when we are experiencing good times, can we remember that they, too, are impermanent? The yin-yang symbol reminds us that everything in life is temporary and that life is eternal change.

- Sit in your favorite meditation posture with a photo or drawing of the yin-yang symbol in front of you.

- Make the intention that you are practicing this meditation to better understand the mysteries of life.

- Focus on your breath for a minute or two to relax your body and quiet your mind.

- Focus your gaze on the symbol and on your breath. If your mind starts to wander, bring your attention back to the symbol and back to your breath.

- If you are new to meditation, try this for about 3 minutes. If you like the practice, over time you can expand the time to 5 minutes, then 10, and then to 15 or 20 minutes.

JUDAISM

Jews are descendents of nomadic Semitic tribes who roamed the Middle East in about 2000 B.C. Abraham, who lived in Mesopotamia in about 1800 B.C., emerged as the leader of this group. God made a covenant with Abraham that his people were God's chosen people. God promised Abraham a permanent home for his tribe in an area called Canaan, now known as Israel. Accordingly, Abraham took his people to this land.

Because of a famine, Abraham's grandson Jacob led his sons and their families to Egypt. Everything went well for the Jews (who called themselves Hebrews) for several centuries until a new Pharaoh forced the Hebrews into slavery.

At this time, a young man named Moses had an experience that changed his life and the course of history for the ancient Jewish people. While herding sheep one day, Moses experienced the presence of God in a burning bush. God told Moses to take his people out of Egypt and back to the land of their ancestors, Canaan. The Pharaoh refused to allow the Hebrews to leave. Moses was directed by God to threaten Egypt with terrible plagues. Egypt was struck with ten plagues before the Pharaoh allowed the Jews to leave.

With both great difficulties and tremendous blessings, Moses led his people to the Promised Land. At one point, God called Moses to Mount Sinai, where he received the Ten Commandments and other ethical teachings, eventually written down as the first five books of the Hebrew Bible (the Old Testament). God entered into a formal covenant with the Jews, once again making them His chosen people.

Judaism gradually evolved and many other prophets helped it grow. In addition to the books of the Bible, written over many centuries, there are commentaries on the Bible and an oral tradition of interpreting the written material.

The theme of exile and redemption is a strong one in Jewish thought, as Jews were at various times enslaved, forbidden to practice their religion, and killed for their beliefs. Jews identify strongly with captive peoples everywhere.

A major Jewish contribution to religious thought is monotheism, the belief in one God. Also fundamental is the concept that God is good. At the time these concepts emerged, the Greeks, Romans, Egyptians, and Babylonians believed in many gods. Their gods were not too different from man, often embodying man's fickle and foolish nature. Unlike these mercurial gods, the Hebrew God was a loving God and took a personal interest in the lives of His people. The Old Testament is full of stories of God telling His people where to live, who to marry, and orchestrating events as lessons. For the Hebrews, direct Divine intervention was the norm.

He was also an ethical God and expected the same of the Hebrews. The Ten Commandments form the basis for our ethical and legal system today. In addition to the Ten Commandments, the Old Testament contains 613 other laws or *mitzvot*. A better definition of *mitzvot* is "good deeds," or perhaps "recommendations to do good deeds." The practice of mitzvot is central to the observant Jew. Important mitzvot, spiritual beliefs, and practices include:

- Godliness: Jews believe that God created human beings in His image. Jews therefore seek to realize godliness in every aspect of life. Realizing godliness means that we make the attributes of

God the norms of humankind. What are the attributes of God? Mercy, kindness, patience, love, honesty, forgiveness, justice (Exodus 34:6-7).

- Loving-Kindness: It is important for Jews to practice kindness, to promote love and community, to open their hearts to all others, and to help those who are less fortunate.

- Observance of the Sabbath: Jews set aside every seventh day for the study of sacred scriptures, prayer, meditation, song, and rest in order to cultivate insight into God, nature, and each other.

In Judaism, these ideal qualities are nurtured through prayer and meditation.

Jewish Meditation

The roots of Jewish meditation are found in the Old Testament: "Be still and know that I am God" (Psalm 46:20) and "Be still before the Lord and wait patiently for Him" (Psalm 37:13). Many Jewish scholars believe that the prophets of the Old Testament waited in silence for Divine guidance — guidance that included practical advice for everyday life and directions for prayer, devotion, and adoration of the Holy One.

The Hebrew word for meditation is *hitbodedut,* which means "being alone with oneself." When we are alone with ourselves in meditation, we open ourselves to an experience of God, the highest possible spiritual experience. Meditation frees us of our ego-based, anthropomorphic concepts of God and opens us to divine knowledge, wisdom, experience, and insight. As we know from the Bible, an encounter with God can be surprising — even alarming. Moses saw God in a burning bush; Isaiah saw God enthroned in the Temple of Jerusalem, accompanied by fiery angels; and Ezekiel saw a radiant figure seated on a throne whirling through the heavens.

Until recently, meditation was the province of a few Jewish scholars. In the late 1970s and early 1980s, Rabbi Aryeh Kaplan, considered the father of modern Jewish meditation, wrote several books on the subject. In doing research, he located many ancient mystical manuscripts. Through diligent efforts, he and others translated these texts and rediscovered a rich tradition of meditation that had been an essential part of Jewish worship in earlier times.

Over the last several years, all Jews have been encouraged to meditate. The practice of meditation may include:

- chanting the names of God

- object meditation — focusing one's attention on a candle, on a flower, or on a card with the holiest name of God written on it

- the recitation of traditional prayers.

SHALOM

(pronunciation: SHAH-LOAM)

Rabbi Ted Falcon, founder of the Bet Alef Meditational Synagogue in Seattle, Washington, and author of *A Journey of Awakening: A Guide for Using the Kabbalistic Tree of Life in Jewish Meditation,* says that he teaches beginning meditators to chant *shalom,* the Hebrew word for "peace." He particularly likes this form of meditation because *shalom* contains the soft "a" sound, which represents the opening of our hearts and minds, and the "o" sound, which grounds us to the earth.

- Sit in your favorite meditation posture.

- Gently close your eyes and focus your inward gaze toward your heart.

- Make the intention that you are practicing this meditation to open your heart and your mind and to enhance your inner peace.

- Focus on your breath for a minute or two to relax your body and quiet your mind.

- Chant *shalom* for about 5 minutes.

Shalom

- Then, silently repeat *shalom* for 3 to 4 minutes, taking the word into your heart and feeling your inner peace emanate through your entire body.

- Lie down and rest for a few minutes.

- As you gain experience in this meditation, extend both the time that you chant and the time that you silently repeat *shalom*, eventually increasing your practice time to 20 to 30 minutes.

CHANTING THE NAME OF GOD

Rabbi Joseph Gelberman recommends this chanting meditation in his book *Physician of the Soul: A Modern Kabbalistic Approach to Health and Healing.* He instructs us to choose one of God's names and chant it for 8 minutes. Here are some of the names, their pronunciations, and their meanings: *Adonai* (pronounced AH-DOE-NAI), my Lord. *El* (pronounced EL), God. *Ein Soph* (pronounced AIN SOF), without end. *Ribbono shel olam* (pronounced RIBO-NO SHEL O-LAM), Master of the Universe. Rabbi Gelberman says that repeating God's name binds you to the spiritual world, and "such binding opens a channel for Divine assistance."

- Sit in your favorite meditation posture.

- Gently close your eyes and focus your inward gaze toward your heart.

- Make the intention that you are practicing this meditation in order to open a channel to the Divine.

- Focus on your breath for a minute or two to relax your body and quiet your mind.

- Choose one of the following names of God and chant for 8 minutes.

- Adonai
- El
- Ein Soph
- Ribbono Shel Olam

- When you are finished, lie down and rest for a few minutes.

CANDLE OR OIL LAMP MEDITATION

Many meditative systems recommend contemplation of a candle flame, but unique to Judaism is the use of a small lamp holding olive oil and a linen wick. In his insightful book, *Jewish Meditation: A Practical Guide,* Rabbi Aryeh Kaplan, considered the father of modern Jewish meditation, explains the difference. "This [type of lamp] would be like the great *menorah* candelabrum that stood in the Jerusalem temple, which may have been used as the object of contemplation. Olive oil has a particularly white flame that draws the gazer into its depths." Try to find such a lamp, but if you can't, use a candle. This meditation is modified from Rabbi Kaplan's.

- Light your lamp or candle in a dark room, making sure that it does not cast a shadow.

- Sit in front of the lamp, gazing at the flame. Allow the flame to fill your entire mind.

- Make the intention that you are practicing this meditation to become more aware of your inner light, your own divine potential.

- Become aware of the colors in the flame: red, yellow, white. Become aware of the heat and the energy radiating from the flame.

- Then become aware of the darkness around the lamp and then the darkness in the room. The darkness can be almost tangible.

- The darkness represents the world around us. The flame or light from the lamp represents our inner light, the spark of divinity within us.

- At the start, meditate for about 5 minutes. As you progress, increase your meditation time to 10 minutes and then to 20 to 30 minutes.

CONTEMPLATING GOD'S MOST SACRED NAME

To Jews, God's most sacred name is the four-letter Tetragrammaton (pronounced TET-RA-GRAM-MA-TON), which we write in English letters as YHVH. It is considered so sacred that it isn't ever pronounced. These four letters have very special meanings in Hebrew. They contain the mystery of charity. According to

The greatest charity that God gives is existence itself. We have no claim to existence and cannot demand that God give it to us as our right. Therefore, when He gives us existence, it is an act of charity. Since this charity is denoted by the Tetragrammaton, the four letters represent the mystery of the creative link between God and man.*

Rabbi Aryeh Kaplan:

This meditation is a slightly modified version of the one found in Rabbi Kaplan's book. By practicing this meditation, we become absorbed in God and gain insight into our unity with the Divine.

- Have a white card with the Tetragrammaton printed on it in thick black ink.

- Sit in your favorite meditation posture and place the card in front of you.

- Gently close your eyes and focus your inward gaze toward your heart.

- Make the intention that you are practicing this meditation in order to become fully absorbed in God.

- Focus on your breath for a minute or two to relax your body and quiet your mind.

- Open your eyes and gaze at the card, contemplating the name.

- If you would like to use a mantra to enhance the practice, you can repeat the mantra

Ribbono shel olam

- When you are finished, lie down and rest for a few minutes.

*Aryeh Kaplan, *Jewish Meditation: A Practical Guide*, Schocken Books, 1995.

Various prayers were once used as meditations, then used as prayers, and are now used as meditations again. The next two meditations are excerpts from the most commonly recited prayers/meditations. They are followed by a modern prayer that incorporates many Jewish ideals.

THE AMIDAH

(pronounced: AM-EE-DAH)

The Amidah is the core of every Jewish prayer service. *Amidah* means "standing." Hayim Halevy Donin explained, "The prayer is called this because it reflects our having stopped to stand in the presence of God."* It contains the basic components of prayer: praising God, petitioning God, and thanking God. The Amidah originally consisted of 18 sections, and is also called the *Shmonei Esrei,* which means "eighteen" in Hebrew. The first blessing, Fathers *(Avot),* is given below.**

- Stand in Tadasana (Mountain Pose), with full awareness of your body (see pages 46 to 47). Stand as still as possible.

- Gently close your eyes or allow your gaze to be cast downward toward a copy of the meditation.

- Make the intention that you are reciting this prayer to praise and thank God.

- Recite the prayer as many times as you like.

Blessed are You, Lord our God and God of our fathers,

God of Abraham, God of Isaac, and God of Jacob,

Great, mighty, and awesome God,

Highest God, doer of good, kind deeds, Master of all,

Who remembers the love of the Patriarchs

And who will bring a redeemer to their children's children

For His name's sake, with love.

King, helper, rescuer, and shield.

Blessed are You, Lord, Shield of Abraham.

* Hayim Halevy Donin, *To Pray as a Jew,* Basic Books, 1980.

THE SHEMA

The Shema is a bedrock Jewish prayer and declaration of faith. This is the first prayer Jews are taught and it is the last thing a Jew is supposed to say before he or she dies. Practicing Jews repeat this prayer twice a day: upon rising in the morning and before retiring in the evening. If you spend a few minutes repeating this prayer, it becomes a mantra. There are several parts to the Shema. The first part is from Deuteronomy 6:4: *Shema Yisrael, Adonai Eloheinu, Adonai echad* (pronunciation: SH'MA YIS-RAY-EL, ADO-NAI EL-O-HAY-NU, ADO-NAI EH-HAD). According to the Torah, *Israel* means "he who contends with the Divine." *Israel* also is a name for the Jewish people. *Adonai* is normally translated as "my Lord," but in a sense, *Adonai* is the term used for what is in fact nameless, the diverse nature of the Oneness of God, the Eternal.

- Sit in your favorite meditation posture.

- Gently close your eyes and focus your inward gaze toward your heart.

- Make the intention that you are practicing this meditation to experience unification with God.

- Focus on your breath for a minute or two to relax your body and quiet your mind.

- Keep your eyes closed or cover your eyes with your right hand (the latter is the traditional prayer posture when reciting the Shema).

- Repeat the prayer aloud, in English or Hebrew, feeling the resonance of the words in your heart and then throughout your whole body. Then bring the meditation into your heart and silently repeat.

- As a beginner, chant the prayer for about 5 minutes. When you bring the meditation into your heart, silently repeat for another 5 minutes. As you progress, increase the two phases of this meditation to 10 minutes each.

Shema Yisrael, Adonai
Elohainu, Adonai echad.

Hear O Israel,
The Eternal is our God,
The Eternal is One.

STRENGTH AND GUIDANCE MEDITATION

This prayer meditation comes from Rabbi Joseph Gelberman's book, *Physician of the Soul*. It embodies the Jewish ideal of developing the attributes of God.

- Sit in your favorite meditation posture.

- Gently close your eyes or cast your gaze downward at a copy of the meditation.

- Make the intention that you are practicing this meditation to develop the attributes of God.

- Focus on your breath for a minute or two to relax your body and quiet your mind.

- Recite the prayer as many times as you would like.

Adonai, Elohim, Oh God

Keep my tongue from evil and my lips from speaking guile.

Be my support when grief silences my voice, and my comfort when woe bends my spirit.

Implant humility in my soul, and strengthen my heart with perfect faith in Thee.

Help me to be strong in temptation and trial and to be patient and forgiving when others wrong me.

Guide me by the light of Thy counsel, that I may ever find strength in Thee, my Rock and Redeemer.*

*Joseph Gelberman and Lesley Sussman, *Physician of the Soul: A Modern Kabbalistic Approach to Health and Healing*, Crossing Press, Inc., May 2000.

CHRISTIANITY

Christians follow the teachings of Jesus Christ, who was born approximately 2000 years ago into a traditional Jewish family in what is now Israel. Little is known of Jesus' early life. He was born in humble surroundings, and it is believed that He learned the trade of carpentry from His father.

During this time, the Roman Empire controlled this land and heavily taxed and oppressed the Jews. In their best efforts to deal with the persecution, the Jewish people splintered into several groups. Also during this period, many Jews fervently anticipated the fulfillment of their scriptures — that God would send a messiah, a savior king, who would deliver them from their oppressors.

When He was around 30, Jesus began a ministry of teaching and healing. His principal message was one of God's overwhelming love for each and every individual. His teachings were not fundamentally different from the message of the Old Testament. He taught that you should love God, love and serve your neighbor, forgive yourself and others, perform works of mercy, and embody all of the attributes of God: mercy, kindness, patience, love, honesty, forgiveness, justice (Exodus 34:6-7). What was different about Christ's message was that He wanted us to include every human being in our definition of neighbor, not just members of our own tribe or faith, and He wanted us to do these things from our hearts, not just because it was the law.

Jesus' extraordinary love and concern for all people teaches us how to live. He counseled all He met, helped people to forgive themselves and others, fed them, healed their physical ailments, and tended to their emotional afflictions. In other words, Christ was the manifestation of God's merciful love. Jesus repeatedly taught that God is within each and every human being. As we open our hearts to the love and mercy God has for us, our lives are transformed and we become vessels through which God's love, mercy, and compassion flows out to everyone we meet.

He so deeply touched His followers with His selfless love, words, and actions that many claimed that Jesus was the long-awaited Messiah. The Greeks called Him "The Christ," meaning "the Anointed One of God" and He is known as Christ — or Jesus Christ — today.

Because Christ's message was so powerful — especially in the age of oppression in which He lived — He became a threat to many governmental and spiritual leaders. Some of them became determined to stop His growing influence. After a betrayal by one of His disciples and a trial, the Romans sentenced Christ to crucifixion — a painful and humiliating death. Upon hearing His sentence, Christ did not seek to save Himself, but instead He surrendered to God's will. He asked God to forgive His killers, knowing that they had acted out of ignorance. Even in suffering and death, Christ showed us how to live. His suffering reminds us that all human beings — including God incarnate — will experience tremendous suffering. Three days after His death, Christ rose from the dead and appeared to His disciples.

God so loved the world that He gave His only Son, that whoever believes in Him should not perish but have eternal life.

— JOHN 3:16

Christian Meditation

Christians believe that Christ died for our sins and that His resurrection represents the new, eternal life man finds through complete surrender to God. Christ's death on the cross also symbolizes our individual need to crucify our ego, the part of us that resists submission to God's will. In surrendering our will to God's will, we too become Christlike. St. Paul wrote: "I have been crucified with Christ; and it is no longer I who live, but it is Christ who lives in me" (Galatians, 2:20).

Though Christians believe that there is only one God, they maintain a belief in the Trinity — God the Father, God the Son, and God the Holy Spirit. Christ is central in this Trinity. Jesus tells us that we must go through Him to reach the Father, and when Jesus appeared to His disciples after His resurrection, "He breathed on them and said, 'Receive the Holy Spirit'" (John 20:22).

Christians believe that God dwells in each and every individual soul. In day-to-day life we are unaware of this divine presence, but through prayer, meditation, and God's grace we can experience God's presence directly. When this occurs, we enter into a mystical state of ecstasy.

Prayer, meditation, and good works purify us of our negative tendencies and help us embody the attributes of God. Through their practice, our hearts open with love and compassion for everyone, even those who make our lives difficult and painful. We naturally start to endure suffering with grace, humility, and detachment. With continued practice, we gain insights into the mystery of God and we experience great joy and inner peace. These spiritual practices, combined with God's grace, help us become "perfect as your Father in heaven is perfect" (Matthew 5:48).

The Eastern Orthodox Church has always recommended meditation to their members, while the Western Church has neither encouraged nor discouraged the practice. Yet some Christians, in various traditions, embraced meditation on their own — by contemplating the words of Jesus, reflecting on the mystery of Christ's passion and resurrection, or by continuous repetition of God's name. Nonetheless, until recently, meditation was primarily the province of a few monks and nuns who committed their lives to full illumination and union with the Divine.

Modern Christian meditation was reinvigorated in the 1960s by Thomas Merton, a Catholic priest and prolific writer, who recommended that "The best way to come to God is to go to your own center and pass through that center into the center of God."* Since then, many Christian leaders have embraced the idea of Centering Prayer (see page 117) and recommend it and the repetition of traditional prayers as meditation practices for all Christians.

*Quoted in Gustave Reininger, *Centering Prayer in Daily Life and Prayer*, Continuum, 1998.

THE JESUS PRAYER

The Jesus Prayer is:

Lord, Jesus Christ, Son of God, have mercy on me.

The Jesus Prayer is from the Eastern Orthodox tradition of Christianity. It mirrors the biblical idea that the name of God is sacred and that with the regular invocation of God's name, we achieve Divine quietness and eventually merge with the Divine. The practice of the Jesus Prayer was popularized by the publication of the *Philokalia* in 1782, an anthology of texts on prayer by various authors.

- Sit or lie down in your favorite meditation posture.

- Gently close your eyes and focus your inward gaze toward your heart.

- Make the intention that you are practicing this meditation to quiet your mind and to merge with the Divine.

- Focus on your breath for a minute or two to relax your body and quiet your mind.

- On the inhalation, silently repeat:

Lord Jesus Christ, Son of God

- On the exhalation, silently repeat:

Have mercy on me.

- Start by repeating the phrase for 5 minutes. As you progress, increase your time to 10 minutes and then to 20 or 30 minutes.

- When you are finished, rest for a few minutes.

CENTERING PRAYER

Christian leaders are now encouraging centering prayer, the silent repetition of one of God's names or one of the many sacred characteristics of God. In the late 1970s, the Catholic priest Father Thomas Keating was disturbed and intrigued that so many young Christians were drawn to TM (Transcendental Meditation) or were going to India to study Hindu and Buddhist meditation practices. In an effort to understand why so many young people were drawn to these practices, Father Keating invited TM teachers and Buddhist monks to his monastery to learn their techniques. He found that mantra meditation techniques were incredibly simple and resulted in powerful spiritual experiences for the practitioner. Father Keating began to offer Christian mantras to his parishioners. The practice quickly spread throughout the Catholic Church and into the Episcopal Church. Now many denominations use this form of meditation.

The essence of Christian centering prayer is mantra meditation or the repetition of one of God's sacred names. Father Keating invites Christians to choose a mantra, one that is a name of God or of a virtue that they would like to nurture in themselves. Here are a few from which to choose:

- Jesus Christ

- My God and my All

- Hail Mary, full of grace

- Jesus, I Trust in You

- The Lord is my shepherd, I shall not want

- Love

- Patience

- Mercy

- Kindness

- Peace

- Sit or lie down in your favorite meditation posture.

- Gently close your eyes and focus your inward gaze toward your heart.

- Make the intention that you are practicing this meditation to unite with God or to develop the virtue you have chosen as your mantra.

- Focus on your breath for a minute or two to relax your body and quiet your mind.

- With your attention at your heart, silently repeat your chosen mantra.

- If possible, synchronize your breath with the mantra. For example, if you have chosen the name of Jesus Christ, on the inhalation silently repeat:

Jesus

and on the exhalation, silently repeat

Christ

- Start by practicing this meditation for 5 minutes. As you progress, increase your time to 10 minutes and then to 20 or 30 minutes.

- When you are finished, rest for a few minutes.

Christians often repeat traditional prayers as a form of meditation. For each of the following meditations, prepare for meditation as you normally do:

- Assume your favorite meditation posture (many Christians prefer kneeling) and quiet your mind with your breath.

- Repeat the prayer as many times as you like, allowing it to deepen your relationship with God.

- When you are finished, be sure to lie down and rest for a few minutes.

THE LORD'S PRAYER

The Lord's Prayer (Matthew 6: 9–13) is a part of all Christian denominations. Of the many Christian leaders with whom I spoke while writing this book, all of them recommended using this prayer as a meditation. By repeating the Lord's Prayer, we imitate Christ and draw ourselves closer to God the Father. As you repeat the prayer, imagine that Christ is in your heart, praying with you.

Our Father, who art in heaven

Hallowed be Thy name.

Thy kingdom come, Thy will be done

On Earth, as it is in heaven.

Give us this day our daily bread.

And forgive us our trespasses, as we forgive those who trespass against us.

And lead us not into temptation, but deliver us from evil.

For Thine is the kingdom, and the power, and the glory, now and forever.

Amen.

THE PRAYER OF ST. FRANCIS

St. Francis was a member of a wealthy family in Assisi, Italy, during the 13th century. After a transformational spiritual experience, Francis left his home and material possessions to live in nature, to help those who were less fortunate than he, and to pray. Soon a group of other young men joined him. They completely relied on God for their material needs. St. Francis may be best known for this prayer, which helps us cultivate our best qualities. As an alternative to repeating the whole prayer, repeat a line or two that are particularly important to you.

Lord, make me an instrument of Thy peace.

Where there is hatred, let me sow love;

where there is injury, pardon;

where there is doubt, faith;

where there is despair, hope;

where there is darkness, light;

where there is sadness, joy.

Oh, Divine Master,

Grant that I may not seek so much to be consoled as to console;

to be understood, as to understand;

to be loved, as to love;

for it is in giving that we receive;

it is in pardoning that we are pardoned;

and it is in dying to self that we are born to eternal life.

NOVENA TO ST. JUDE

Novenas are prayers that are said for nine days when petitioning God for a certain intention.

Jude Thaddeus was Christ's cousin and one of the Twelve Apostles. St. Jude is known as the Patron Saint of lost or impossible causes, and of desperate situations. If you find yourself in such a predicament, recite this prayer once daily for 9 days in a row. After saying the prayer, repeat The Lord's Prayer five times.

Most holy Apostle, St. Jude, faithful servant and friend of Jesus, the Church honors and invokes you universally, as the patron of difficult cases, of things almost despaired of. Pray for me, I am so helpless and alone. Intercede with God for me that He bring visible and speedy help where help is almost despaired of. Come to my assistance in this great need that I may receive the consolation and help of heaven in all my necessities, tribulations, and sufferings, particularly — *(make your request here)* — and that I may praise God with you and all the saints forever. I promise, O Blessed St. Jude, to be ever mindful of this great favor granted me by God and to always honor you as my special and powerful patron, and to gratefully encourage devotion to you. Amen.

ISLAM

*The best jihad [struggle] is by the one who strives
against his own self for Allah.*

— MUHAMMAD

The Arabic word *Islam* is derived from the word *salaam*, which means "peace," but in a secondary sense it means "surrender." Its full connotation is "the perfect peace that comes when one's life is surrendered to God."* In Arabic, *Allah* means "the God" and in Islam there is only one God. *Muslim* means "one who submits."

Muhammad, the prophet of Islam, was born in approximately 570 A.D. in Mecca. It was a time earmarked by political chaos, tribal warfare, economic hardship, and moral decay. At that time, there were more than 360 gods worshipped in Arabia, Allah being only one of these. Idol worship was prevalent, and most people believed in desert demons and evil spirits.

Muhammad's father died two months before his birth, his mother died when he was 6, and his grandfather, who had become his guardian after his mother's death, died when he was 9. Muhammad then went to live with his uncle. These personal hardships sensitized Muhammad to the suffering of others and made him always willing to help the poor and less fortunate.

As an adult in search of solitude, Muhammad began visiting a cave just outside of Mecca. On one visit, a voice within the cave spoke to Muhammad and said:

La ilaha illa Allah!
There is no God but Allah.

Further visits to the cave brought more instruction from the voice, which belonged to the Angel Gabriel, who was speaking for God. After a while, Muhammad began teaching others what the angel had taught him about Allah.

Muslims believe that Muhammad was the final prophet of God, the one God of the Jews and the Christians. For this reason, Muhammad is called "the seal of the prophets." Muslims accept the prophets of both the Old and the New Testament, including Abraham, Moses, and Jesus, who revealed important concepts: monotheism, the Ten Commandments, and the Golden Rule. Muslims believe that Muhammad clarified the teachings of the previous prophets and revealed the Five Pillars of Islam, which are principles to live by. The Five Pillars are:

The Proclamation of Faith *(Shahada)*: "There is no God but Allah and Muhammad is his prophet."

Formal Prayer *(Salat)*: This obligatory prayer, which contains verses from the Quran, must be recited at dawn, noon, mid-afternoon, sunset, and before retiring.

Charity and Kindness *(Zakat)*: Muslims must be kind to others, perform good works, and help others in any way they can. Muslims in the middle and upper income brackets must annually give 2.5% of their income and one-fortieth of their assets to the poor.

Fasting during Ramadan *(Sawm)*: During Ramadan, the Islamic holy month, Muslims must fast and avoid drink, tobacco, and sexual intimacy from sunrise to sunset. After sunset, moderation is advised. Ramadan also provides the opportunity for Muslims to practice controlling their emotions. During this holy time, Muslims must refrain from all arguing and displays of anger.

Pilgrimage to Mecca *(Hajj)*: All Muslims who are physically and financially able must visit the holy city at least once and perform the requisite rituals.

*Huston Smith, *The World's Religions*.
**Note: In Islam, the idea of God is so sacred that the word isn't fully written out. Traditionally it is written as G'd in English. For clarification and simplicity, in many cases in this text I have not used that form. In the specific meditations, however, I do use the traditional form.

Islamic Meditation

It is the first two pillars of faith that brought Muslims to meditation. The daily prayers, Salat in Arabic, are repeated 5 times each day and are the most essential observance of Islam. Furthermore, Muslims repeat the Profession of Faith, or Shahada, many times per day. These prayers are obligatory, but many other prayers and meditations are recommended.

SUFISM

The mystical school of Islam is Sufism. Sufis are God-drunken lovers, divinely intoxicated on the elixir of their love for their Beloved Allah. The Sufis believe that each of us has a soul that is a spark of the Divine. The individual Sufi soul so longs for union with the Divine that his entire life is devoted to that cause. They rage with passion when their Beloved abandons them and cry tears of joy when He returns. Miracles are commonplace. For Sufis, the veil of illusion has been lifted — they see behind the veil of illusion that separates man from God and man from his neighbor.

Rumi is the most famous of all Sufis. Jalaluddin Rumi was born in 1207 in what is now Afghanistan. He died in 1273 in what is today Turkey. Rumi was a philosopher and mystic of Islam, but he was not an orthodox Muslim. To Rumi, all religions and paths to God are valid. Rumi's doctrine of unlimited tolerance, positive reasoning, goodness, charity and awareness through love has appealed to people of all spiritual backgrounds. Rumi is best remembered for his poetry, which inspires love for God and our fellow man.

Sufi Dancing as Meditation

When most of us think of Sufism, Whirling Dervishes come to mind. This type of dance, called *sema,* was both an inspiration of Rumi's and an outgrowth of Turkish customs. Sema represents a mystical journey of man's spiritual ascent through love to Perfection. Through the dance, the dancer turns or whirls toward Absolute Truth. He abandons his ego or self-will. In fact, the hat the Dervish wears represents his ego's tombstone and the white skirt represents the ego's shroud. It is only by abandoning our ego, our self-identification, that we can find union with the Divine. This state of ecstasy is called *Fenafillah.* However, the idea is not to stay in this state of unbroken ecstasy. Having achieved union with Allah for a brief time, the Dervish finishes his dance and returns to his earthly role — a servant to God, to his Prophet, and to his fellow man.

The sema ends with a reading from the Quran, usually the following verse from Sura al-Bakara (The Cow) 2, verse 115: "Unto God belong the East and the West, and whichever way ye turn, you are faced with Him. He is All-Embracing and All Knowing." Then there is a prayer for the repose of all prophets and believers.

DHIKR: REMEMBRANCE OF G'D

(pronunciation: THI-KER)

Many Muslims practice a form of meditation known as *dhikr*, the remembrance of Allah or G'd. There are 99 names for Allah, each invoking a different aspect of G'd. You can count the prayers on your right hand or you can use dhikr beads or prayer beads. Listed below are a few of the most commonly chanted names of Allah.

- Sit in your favorite meditation pose.

- Gently close your eyes and focus your inward gaze toward your heart.

- Choose one of Allah's names.

- Make the intention that you are practicing this meditation to praise Allah.

- Focus on your breath for a minute or two to relax your body and quiet your mind.

- Start chanting Allah's name, feeling the name resonate in your heart.

- After a few minutes, silently repeat the name for another 5 minutes. Continue to focus on your heart.

- When you have finished, lie down and rest.

- As you progress in this meditation, extend both the period of chanting and silent meditation.

Allah (AL-LAH)

Ar-Rahman (AR-RAH-MAN): The Most Compassionate, the Beneficent

Ar-Rahim (AR RA-HEEM): The Merciful

Ash Shahid (ASH SHA-HEED): The Witness

Ar-Razzaq (AR RA-ZAK): The Provider

Al-Muhaymin (AL MU-HII-MEN): The Protector

Al-Hakim (AL HA-KEEM): The Wise

Al-Wadud (AL WA-DUUD): The Loving One

Al-Haqq (AL HAK): The Truth

AL-Mu'Min (AL MU-MEEN): The Granter of Security

At the first stage one recites the name of God with one's tongue; then when the heart becomes alive one recites inwardly with the heart.

—ABD AL-QADIR AL-JILANI

Dhikr meditations that appeal to Muslims and to non-Muslims are listed below. These sacred phrases should be chanted 33 times each.

Glory be to G'd

Praise be to G'd

G'd is the greatest

There is no goal but G'd.

THE SHAHADA

The Shahada is the First Pillar of Islam. Muhammad recommended that his fellow Muslims repeat this phrase constantly. The first part of the Shahada is: La ilaha illa Allah! (pronounced: LA ILAHA IL'ALLAH).* Using it as a mantra makes perfect sense.

La ilaha illa Allah!

or

There is no god but G'd!

*The next part of the Shahada affirms that Muhammad is the prophet of Allah.

- Sit in your favorite meditation pose.

- Gently close your eyes and focus your inward gaze toward your heart.

- Make the intention that you are practicing this meditation to praise Allah.

- Focus on your breath for a minute or two to relax your body and quiet your mind.

- Start to chant the mantra, either in Arabic or in English, feeling the energy of the mantra in your heart.

- After a few minutes, silently repeat the name for another 5 minutes. Continue to focus on your heart.

- When you have finished, lie down and rest.

- As you progress in this meditation, extend both the period of chanting and silent meditation.

TAJWID

(pronounced TAJ-WEED)

Tajwid is the recitation of the Quran. Both Muslims and non-Muslims find listening to the recitation of the Quran to be very soothing. Many Muslims who practice tajwid learn particular verses; others start at the beginning of their sacred text. Memorization and recitation of the Quran is highly valued. Recitations are normally in Arabic but we have provided the translations.

The most recited verse in the Quran is *Al-Fatihah* ("the Opening"), which is the opening verse of the Quran. Muslims say this prayer at least 17 times a day during the 17 *rakats*, or units of their daily obligatory *Salat* (prayers). This verse is often used as the opening or closing of a meeting or gathering.

Another commonly recited verse is *Al-Ikhlas,* meaning "Sincerity."

To use these verses as meditations, follow the instructions below.

- Sit in your favorite meditation pose.

- Gently close your eyes and focus your inward gaze toward your heart, or cast your gaze downward toward a copy of the verse.

- Make the intention that you are practicing this meditation to praise Allah.

- Focus on your breath for a minute or two to relax your body and quiet your mind.

- Recite the verse as many times as you like.

- When you are finished, lie down and rest for a few minutes.

AL-FATIHAH (THE OPENING)

(pronunciation: AL-FA-TEE-HA)

- To prepare, follow the general instructions at left.

- Recite the following prayer as many times as you like.

In the Name of Allah, Most Merciful, Most Kind:

Praise be to Allah, Lord of the worlds,

Most Merciful, Most Compassionate,

Master of the Day of Judgment.

You alone we worship, You alone we ask for help.

Guide us in the straight path,

The path of those on whom You have poured forth Your grace,

Not the path of those who have incurred Your wrath,

Nor of those who have gone astray.

AL-IKHLAS (SINCERITY)

(pronunciation: AL-IKH-LAS)

- To prepare, follow the general instructions at left.

- Recite the following prayer as many times as you like.

In the name of Allah, Most Merciful, Most Kind:

Say: He is Allah, The One.

Allah is Eternal.

He begets not, and He is not begotten.

And there is none equal to Him.

THE HEART AS A MIRROR

I learned this meditation many years ago from my friend David Bierman. I did not know it was of Sufi origin until I read Neil Douglas-Klotz's superb book, *Desert Wisdom* (Harper Collins, 1995). Not long after reading his book, I found a quote from Abd al-Qadir al-Jilani, a Sufi mystic. This quote explains the source of the meditation.

- Sit or lie down in your favorite meditation posture.

- Gently close your eyes and focus your inward gaze toward your heart.

- Make the intention that you are practicing this meditation to open your heart to the Divine.

- Focus on your breath for a minute or two to relax your body and quiet your mind.

- Focus on your heart. Imagine that your heart is a mirror and with each breath, the mirror of your heart becomes increasingly clear.

- Become aware of your heart as a sacred space, an altar to God and to your own inner light.

- See that your heart is completely clear and reflecting back to you your deepest desires, your true self.

- With your clean mirror, what do you see? What images of Allah, the One, do you see? What images of your Divine self do you see?

- Do not be afraid of what you might see — everything is Divine.

Dear friend, your heart is a polished mirror. You must wipe it clean of the veil of dust that has gathered upon it, because it is destined to reflect the light of divine secrets. When the light from Allah, [who is] the light of the heavens and the earth, begins to shine upon the regions of your heart, the lamp of the heart will be lit.... It is your private sun, for you are the one whom Allah guides....

A Final Word

In writing this book, my intention has been to make meditation as easy and accessible as possible. Most of us are overly busy and find it difficult to make time for meditation. Yet the busier we are, the more we need to meditate so we can reconnect to our inner harmony, love, and joy.

To say that our world is extremely stressful is an understatement. Often we are unaware of how bombarded we are with stimulants to our nervous system — business deadlines, taking care of our families, noise, traffic, billboards, negative headlines. We often need to "be on guard," which triggers the "fight or flight" mode and drains our energy. Even the activities we enjoy can result in fatigue and stress.

Our anxiety, stress, and fatigue can make us sick and can negatively impact our relationships. Meditation gives us the opportunity to prepare for the day ahead so we can greet it with equanimity and joy. At the end of the day, meditation allows us to unwind from our physical, emotional, and mental stress. Meditation allows us to reconnect to our hearts and to our innate serenity, peace, love, kindness, and compassion. We need to be peaceful and happy, both for ourselves and to help others feel peaceful. Our energies influence those around us. Meditation is a gift we give to ourselves, yet our loved ones and co-workers become the mutual beneficiaries. As we become balanced and joyful we are able to be the best that we can be — and we can then give others our very best.

We must take a few minutes each day to be silent. In music, the notes and the silence between the notes create the rhythm. Our lives can only be truly beautiful if we have periods of activity and periods of rest. The silence of meditation provides that rest on a very deep level. And in the midst of that silence we may have the good fortune to gain insights into ourselves and into the mystery of life. It is impossible for me to address all the great benefits you may experience from a meditation practice. But wouldn't it be fun to find out?

Index

*Names of meditations and postures are italicized.